MERIDIAN

MERIDIAN

by
KIJA KIM

CLARK HILL PUBLICATIONS

This book is memoir. It reflects the author's present recollections of experiences over time. Some names and characteristics have been changed, some events have been compressed, and some dialogue has been recreated.

Map of Chosen (Korea) courtesy of the Harvard Map Collection, Harvard Library. Figure 3, Korean Funeral 1947, licensed from Bridgeman Images. All other photos are from the author.

ISBN (hardcover) 979-8-9903106-0-5
ISBN (paperback) 979-8-9903106-1-2
ISBN (epub) 979-8-9903106-2-9

Book Design by Maureen Forys, Happenstance Type-O-Rama

TABLE OF CONTENTS

PART ONE

PART TWO

PART THREE

MAP OF CHOSEN (KOREA)

PART ONE

THE KOREAN WAR

"I am looking for a little place that may be around here. A long time ago, it was called Ilwon-ri. Do you know it by any chance?" I asked the hotel concierge, a young man in a handsome uniform at the InterContinental Seoul Hotel. My heart was racing in anticipation of finding the place.

I stayed at the hotel as one of fifteen advisors to Park Geun-hye, the 11th president of the Republic of Korea, the first woman to be Korea's president, and the first female president elected as head of state in East Asia. I was the only Korean American to be selected to advise on her three-year

Figure 1. My first meeting with President Park, Los Angeles, 2013. Official Blue House photo.

plan for Economic Innovation—what an incredible opportunity and honor!

I had indeed returned to Korea *in a golden robe*, as I promised my father when I left for America a lifetime ago.

The soaring three-story lobby was crowded with locals and international hotel guests. The hotel could have been in any international city.

"Oh, it must be Ilwon-dong, now. Why?" he asked, looking at me blankly.

"It was where our family escaped during the Korean War. Can you tell me how I can get there?" I asked excitedly. *What if I find the place? What if it is still there? What would it be like? Would there be anything left that I remembered?*

The concierge interrupted my thoughts.

"There is nothing there to see. The only famous building there is the Samsung Hospital. Other than that, there are only high-rise apartment buildings." He looked at me strangely.

~~

We heard strange rumblings outside. It was early in the morning on June 25, 1950.

The tanks were rolling into the streets of Seoul. I was in third grade. My parents told us to stay home and not go outside. It was a surprise attack—that's how the Korean War started.

North Korean soldiers occupied Seoul within hours and pushed down to Busan—the southernmost city in South Korea—within days without resistance.

There were occasional gunshots.

"What is that noise?" we asked, all scared.

Our parents were worried and whispered together in hushed tones so as not to frighten us. Later, I found out the shots we heard were executions.

Our family lived in a college town, Dongsoong-dong, behind Seoul National University. My parents suspected some communist sympathizers in the university who might cheer on the North Korean invasion. *Who knows, they could be our neighbors?*

Even though my father was in the construction business, not a professor, my parents thought it would be too dangerous for us to stay in Seoul. In addition, there were rumors that the ruthless North Korean soldiers would execute anyone in sight. The war in Ukraine today, and the discovery of mass graves there bring back all these memories.

My parents, my three siblings, and I fled quietly during the night on foot, heading to the countryside carrying minimal supplies, leaving behind our comfortable home and our beloved grandmother, who was too frail to make the journey with us. Late into the night, we arrived at a small farming village, Ilwon-ri, south of the Han River.

The village had a small community center, about two dozen farmhouses with thatched roofs scattered around, and a nearby town well. On the outskirts of the village, watermelon farms and rice paddies were separated by narrow dirt dikes to hold the water between them. The dikes were so narrow and slippery that I almost fell into the rice paddy where there were leeches in the water. Some terraced rice paddies were on the hills, and others were in the flat areas with small reservoirs here and there to supply water to the fields.

We initially stayed with several other refugee families in the community center, a small hall. We stayed there for the first few days until we moved into a room rented from a local family.

We roamed the country with no schools to go to during the day. My sister Kisoo and I sometimes followed the village women to pick wild dandelions and field onions. Other times, we gathered the firewood in nearby mountains and brought it home. There were also watermelon fields nearby, and one morning, my sister and I snuck into a field, picked a melon, and put it in her canvas school bag.

"Hey, you kids, get out of here! I am coming down to get you!" the watchman yelled at us from the *Won Du Muck,* a hut built like a treehouse. We were careful tiptoeing and bending down low at the edge of the field, but we got caught. We were scared to death and ran as fast as we could. But the watermelon was too heavy, and the bag handle broke. We dropped the melon.

"I want that watermelon!" I stopped running to pick up the shattered pieces.

"Forget the watermelon. Just keep running!" my sister yelled, clutching her broken school bag and pushing me to run. So, with no melon to bring home, we ran.

Early one morning, I woke up to find my father and brother gone. *What happened to them?* Mother said they went further south to be safe from the North Korean soldiers. My brother was only in his early teens, but apparently, my father feared that any male captured would be forced to join the North Korean army. Furthermore, it was dangerous for men to stay long in one place. And they simply disappeared.

After Father and brother left, Mother often snuck home to Seoul to check on Grandmother. It took Mom all day to cross the Han River and return to our house. Each time, she brought things to exchange for food with the locals. Once, she had lovely silk fabrics she had saved for her dresses, and other times, she brought fine china and crystals that were only used for special occasions. Anything she could think of to exchange for food.

I was sorry to see such nice things given away, which we would never get back. I especially missed the beautiful hand-carved wooden bowl we filled with apples, pears, and persimmons in the fall. It reminded me of my birthday in November. My father always bought persimmons, my favorite fruit, on my birthdays.

Those things also made me think of New Year's Day, the biggest holiday in Korea. Before the war, girls wore beautiful silk dresses and Korean costumes on New Year's Day, with long red skirts and yellow or green blouses with rainbow-striped sleeves. My mom used to take out the best china and crystal for New Year's dinner. It was always a banquet with many dishes, especially dumpling soups and rice cakes for visiting relatives. During the day, we visited our relatives to do *Sebai*, a unique bow, kneeling and bowing our heads down to the floor. We wished them much *luck and fortune in the New Year*. In return, we received money, usually newly printed, symbolizing a new beginning. We always remembered who gave us the most money and counted it like Halloween candies.

Whenever my mother left to go back to Seoul, my sister and I went to the river's edge to wait for her return. We'd stay all day, sometimes till dusk. One day, my mother didn't come back. So, we went home alone late in the evening by ourselves.

We waited for Mom every day. Finally, we were alone and awake, thinking of Mom at night. *Where is she now? What happened to her? Did the North Korean soldiers capture her? Is she ever going to come back?* We cried quietly in despair. *What would happen to us if she didn't come back?*

About a week later, she suddenly appeared at the door, tired and drained. We ran out crying for happiness, embracing her tight, not to let her go away again. I don't remember how we survived that long without our mom. My sister was only in the sixth grade and in charge of us.

After many tears, we finally sat in the room and listened to the story of her harrowing escape. On her way back from Seoul, she had been captured by the North Korean soldiers and taken to the labor camp, a peach orchard, to pick peaches day after day. There were primarily women like herself. She worried about us alone, starving. Planning the escape, she paid careful attention to the patterns of their breaks. Finally, she snuck out during one of the soldier's breaks, escaped from the labor camp, risking her life, and found her way back to us. The whole time, she survived by eating only peaches.

Shortly after my mother's return, I went to the town well near the community center to get a bucket of water. I tried to grab the water bucket hanging on the pulley, but it was too far to reach, and I fell into the well. I could not see the outside, only the top of the pulley.

"Help! Help!" I screamed for a long time. Finally, several local men ran to the well, talking loudly. And someone jumped into the well, lifted and pulled me out. I trembled with fear, but luckily, there wasn't too much water, and I didn't drown.

But the townspeople were furious that I contaminated the village's only water source. So they had to drain and clean the entire well. I then became known by the whole village as 'the refugee kid who fell into the well.'

President Syngman Rhee pleaded to the U.N. for help when the North Korean soldiers invaded South Korea in June 1950. Soon, Allied soldiers led by the United States came to our aid.

In September 1950, General Douglas MacArthur, the commander of U.N. forces, landed at Incheon near Seoul—the site of Incheon International Airport today—and advanced into North Korea, pushing through a disintegrating North Korean army toward the Yalu River, the border with China. Soon after their arrival, the Allied soldiers recaptured Seoul.

By September 28th that year, thinking the war was over, the South Korean government had officially allowed refugees to return to Seoul. It could've been September or October, as I remember it was getting cold. My mom, sisters, and I left the village, our wartime home, and returned to Seoul.

We were surprised to see that our father and brother were already there. We didn't know their whereabouts for the whole summer, and I missed them a lot. I often wondered what they were doing and if I would ever see them again.

After the joyful reunion, we all sat down. We listened quietly to how Father and my brother wandered around every day in different places so they wouldn't get caught by the North Koreans, sometimes sleeping in a *Won Du Muck,* but mostly camping. Then, as soon as my father heard that it was safe to return to Seoul, they came home and waited for us. Finally, our entire family was reunited.

My mother cooked a huge pumpkin porridge on the first day home. It might have been the only thing available in quantity after the war. Everyone, including my grandmother, sat on the floor around a big, round, low dining table and prayed, thanking God for our family's safe return and for providing this food. It was the most delicious meal I had tasted in a long time.

I couldn't stop eating. Finally, I ate so much of it that I spread out on the floor and announced, "I can't move."

Everyone laughed, and the incident became family folklore—we still laugh about it to this day! It felt to me like *Chooseok,* Thanksgiving Day in Korea, which falls on August 15th, the harvest moon in the moon calendar.

We also learned many neighbors lost someone from their families—either killed or kidnapped to the North, and never saw them again. I had a good friend whose father was abducted to the North and never returned. We were so fortunate that everyone in our family survived. When the schools finally reopened, the Allied soldiers were still stationed at my elementary school, so I had to go to a school in a neighboring town, and we had combined classes with different teachers.

Our return home didn't last long. By November of that same year, the Chinese army crossed the Yalu River into North Korea and entered the war. The 300,000-man Chinese army offensive caught U.N. forces off guard, pushed through the south, and recaptured Seoul. So began the second retreat on January 4, 1951.

We had to flee again. It was a chaotic time; everyone tried to escape. Us kids were anxious, asking our parents, "All the neighbors have left. When are we leaving?"

"The baby's navel hasn't healed yet. We need to wait a little longer," Mom said. My baby sister, Kimyung, was born in late October, and my mother was concerned it was too early to make the long trek with a tiny newborn in tow.

Unfortunately, we missed the last train leaving Seoul to the south, and there were no other means of transportation to flee from Seoul. We were desperate. Somehow, my father acquired a wagon. We hurriedly packed suitcases and loaded them in the wagon.

"I am not staying," my grandmother declared. "I am going with you this time."

And so, she came, sitting tentatively on top of the luggage.

Our entire family walked among thousands of refugees through the bitterly cold winter. My father and older brother, Kigap, then only fifteen, took turns pulling the wagon, and my mother carried our baby sister, not yet twelve weeks old, on her back. My older sister, Kisoo (eleven), me (eight), and my younger sister, Kiok (four), all walked. From time to time, Kiok got too tired to walk and hopped on the wagon with Grandma. I was exhausted from walking, too, but I couldn't ask to ride on the wagon. Even at that age, I knew I was too big, and it was too much to ask.

We stopped at empty houses at nightfall, sharing tight spaces with other refugees. Then, at sunrise, we started walking again. We were constantly afraid of the invading Chinese and North Korean soldiers catching up to us. After about a week of walking, we finally stopped in Ansung. It was only about forty-two miles south of Seoul, but felt like hundreds of miles. After that, we could not go any further. We were just too tired!

Ansung was eerily empty, like a ghost town, because the townspeople had evacuated further south. We temporarily occupied one of the empty houses to wait and see. My parents were nervous, especially at night. The Allied soldiers were retreating, and we didn't know how near the invading soldiers were.

Another refugee family from Seoul stopped at a nearby house. They had a couple of older teenage girls. Shocked at their strange appearances, I asked, "Mom, why did the girls shave their hair and dress like boys?"

"Their parents made them look like boys to keep them safe from marauding soldiers, whether Allied or Chinese/ North Koreans," she answered. I didn't ask further, but it scared me.

Fortunately, the North Koreans had come close but never reached Ansung, and we settled there for a while. Shortly afterward, the owner of the house we were occupying returned. He was surprised to see us living in his home. In addition, I was wearing a pair of brown and white Oxford shoes I found in the house without asking anyone—I guess no one in my family had noticed! The owner accused us of stealing them, and my father explained and begged, and he let us temporarily stay in separate quarters. Of course, I got in BIG trouble. There were other refugee families from Seoul in town; we were all going through the war together.

The house was a prominent Korean-style stucco house with a black tile roof. It was the only tiled roof in town—the others were thatched. There was a courtyard in the center of the house with big double-wooden gates, and each room had rice-papered doors facing into the courtyard. The area where we stayed was likely the servants' quarters.

Of course, there was no school to attend again. By spring, we had missed school for several months. I roamed the countryside all day, digging wild vegetables with the locals and hiking the mountains with my sister Kisoo—just like we did the first time we fled Seoul. While hiking, I accidentally hit a beehive and got stung all over! I screamed, shaking my arms hysterically. It felt like there were thousands of bees attacking me. My face, neck, and arms were all swollen. The locals advised my mom to put soybean paste and miso on the stings. Miraculously, it relieved the pain. What a wise ancient Korean remedy it was!

In April 1951, President Harry S. Truman relieved (fired) General Douglas MacArthur of his command of the U.S. forces in Korea. At the height of the war, Truman's action shocked America and and astonished the world.

By late spring of 1951, the Allies had again driven the North Korean and Chinese soldiers out of Seoul and pushed them back to the North, but the South Korean government still didn't allow civilians to return. They made a mistake in having the civilians return home too early last time, and the war was still going on. So now, they were very cautious. Nonetheless, my father was anxious to get home, and in the summer of 1951, he left Ansung for Seoul with my brother to scout out the situation and decided to remain in Seoul, staying at our house.

A couple of months later, in late fall, my mom said, "Your dad needs company, and he wants you to come."

Perhaps I was the perfect candidate because my mom needed my older sister, Kisoo, to babysit our younger sister and the baby.

My mom arranged our travel, leaving my sisters and grandmother behind. But it might have been my mom's idea to send me since I didn't know how they could communicate without mail or a phone.

When I left, Kisoo was sad, following me to the road and waving goodbye. She was only in the sixth grade but always responsible and protective of me—like a little mother more than a sister. I looked back, and she stood frozen—her loose dress hung over her thin frame.

We went everywhere, especially during the war, with me following her around. We were buddies. Later, on one of her rare visits to Seoul, my mom brought a letter from my sister about *how much she missed me and how she cried for days after I left,* which made me miss her all over again.

Mom and I traveled by bus to a safe house near the Han River. Several others were already there, waiting to cross the river south of Seoul. I didn't see any children—only adults, primarily men. I was hungry, and a woman innkeeper served us a simple dinner of rice and soup. My mom and I ate dinner quietly among the strangers watching us curiously, a woman and child traveling together.

It was still illegal to go back to Seoul, and we had to stay until nightfall when the smuggler's boat signaled us to come on board. I was tired and had fallen asleep after the long journey. It must have been after midnight. My mom tried to wake me up to get on the boat, but I was in a dead sleep and couldn't move. Even today, when I have to wake up in the middle of the night to go somewhere, I think of that night and how dreadful it was dragging myself up to not to miss the boat, still half-asleep and shivering.

My mother said that the smuggler was reluctant to have a child (me) on board, and she begged him and warned me, "You must be quiet no matter what happens. If not, you will put others in danger." There was a rumor that a smuggler had to throw a baby in the river because the baby cried. It scared me to death. In the dead of night, we crossed the river, quietly holding our breath. The only sound was the gentle rippling of water from the slow rowing, but we made it to the landing. At last, we were going home to see my father!

When my mom and I arrived at our house in Seoul, I was surprised to see a neighbor, a widow, helping Dad and my brother with the cooking.

The neighborhood was quiet, and nobody seemed to be around. The woman was dressed in a simple Korean dress with a long gray-wrapped skirt and a white linen blouse; she looked plain and older than my mom and didn't talk much. She almost ignored us, just working around in the kitchen. I didn't know how long she had been there, but she could have been a hired cook or, perhaps, volunteered to help my father since only a few neighbors had returned.

My mother stayed a few days and left for Ansung, where we escaped the war, leaving me behind with my Dad and brother. She hugged me tight and said, "Be good. Help your Dad and brother." Then she was gone! I was sad to see her go.

And shortly after my arrival, the neighbor woman left, too. Maybe she didn't like me or thought we didn't need her help anymore, even though I was only eight years old and didn't know how to cook. I didn't miss her though because she wasn't friendly. I didn't know who she was and wondered if my mom had sent me to spy on her.

Now, it was just the three of us: Dad, my brother, and me. During the day, I kept myself busy trying to find something to do that could help Dad.

We lived in the Seoul National University neighborhood before and after the war. The U.S. military, the 5th Air Force, occupied the entire Medical School compound nearby, and my brother got a job as a houseboy. He was fifteen, high school age, but had no school to go to. There, he learned English and became fluent, which was helpful when he came to America many years later.

My brother brought the soldier's laundry home for ironing so we could earn some money. They paid in U.S. dollars, and Dad became an expert at pressing shirts. Then, one day, my brother brought an electric iron home for us. It was the first time we had seen one, shining stainless steel with a thick, black-and-white tweeded cord, like a jump rope, attached.

However, my Dad had to heat it on a charcoal stove because we lacked electricity. Still, we were so proud to have an electric iron!

Sometimes, when I was bored, I went to the gate of the Medical School building and waited for my brother. Some of the G.I.s gave me candies or chewing gum, and I was happy. Then, when my brother came out after work, I showed him my booty, and we walked home together.

We lived through a severely cold winter in 1951. When it was safe to return the following summer, my father finally went to Ansung to bring the rest of the family back home. Once again, our family was reunited after the prolonged war. That was a long, long time ago, over seventy years. However, the Korean War never ended. The country is still divided between North and South and has been since the end of World War II. Under the Korean Armistice Agreement of 1953, an agreement between North Korea, China, and the United Nations Command, all sides simply ceased fire and established a Demilitarized Zone (DMZ) to serve as a buffer zone between North and South Korea.

My brother, Kigap, is now retired south of West Palm Beach, Florida. He worked for many years for a company making an industrial diamond compound in Rochester, New York, and became the company's president years ago. When he and his wife, Ilsun, visited me in Naples, Florida, we discussed wartime and reminisced about the old days. Ilsun chimed in, "Your brother often talked about you during the war and felt sorry. Your hands had frostbite and were all roughed up. You were so little and still tried to help. Once you went down the hill to a well to get water, and coming back, you fell. Your arms and knees were all bleeding and raw, but you didn't cry. Your brother still feels painful about it."

Somehow, I had forgotten it, but my brother's memory helped me to remember another incident. Dad asked me to bring back an iron mortar and pestle he had borrowed from a neighbor. It was so heavy that my arms felt like breaking off, but I was afraid to put it down, thinking if I dropped it, I might break it. When I got home, my nose bled, which I have never forgotten.

MY EARLIEST MEMORY

Before the Korean War, my father had a farm in Yeoncheon, a small farming village about thirty miles north of Seoul.

Our family lived in Seoul, but we spent the summers in Yeoncheon. I fondly remember the farm—there were creeks and mountains, and women washed their

Figure 2. My parents with children (L to R) Kigap, Kija, Kisoo

clothes at the river's edge. During the summer, I roamed around the peach orchard with a cousin, a boy my age. Being the youngest child of our family, I spent more time there than my school-aged brother and sister.

My grandparents lived on the farm year-round. Besides farming the land for us, our caretaker and tenant farmer's family also cared for our grandparents. It was a Korean-style house with a thatched roof, stucco walls, rice-papered doors, and radiant heat—first invented in Korea—on all bedroom floors. A courtyard was in the middle with a big, black iron knocker on a thick wooden gate.

One of my earliest memories was when my grandfather died. My mother told me later that I would have been three years old.

Strangers were coming and going throughout the days, and some went into my grandfather's bedroom with my father and uncle, where his body was kept.

The children were shooed away from the house. But my curiosity led me to the window outside my grandfather's bedroom. I was too short to reach the window, so my cousin and I gathered some rocks to stand on. I licked my fingers repeatedly, dampening the rice paper to not make a popping sound, and peeped in.

What a shocking scene! The men wrapped my grandfather's body like a mummy, with a white cloth resembling the gauze you wrap around wounds, while my father and uncle looked on. I was breathless. I couldn't take my eyes off it.

I warned my cousin, "You must be quiet. If not, we will get into trouble." But my cousin was anxious to see what was going on. "It's my turn! Let me look, too." His whispering got my father's attention, and he turned toward the window. I jumped down quickly, and my cousin never had his turn.

The weather was warm on the funeral day, and the fields and mountains were green. The whole village came out for the funeral procession to a hill in the mountains where my father had a private family cemetery plot. The mourners, both men and women alike, wore white funeral clothes made of hemp fabric and shoes made of straw. The men wore tall hats made of hemp.

The pallbearers led the procession through dirt roads and up to the mountains, winding through narrow rice paddies and a bridge over the river. Women followed, balancing food in big, wooden bowls on their heads. They put a round disk-like pad on their head for cushion and

Figure 3. Korean funeral procession, circa 1947

balancing, and some walked without touching the bowl. My cousin and I followed them at the end of the long procession. Rice, fish, fruits, and rice cakes were offered at the grave so my dead grandfather would not be hungry on his final journey to heaven.

~~~

After the Korean War, our farm was too close to the new Demilitarized Zone (DMZ), a demarcation line separating North and South Korea. The South Korean government only granted access to the military and initially denied landowners and residents entry. As a result, my father and family lost access to our farm and land in the mountains.

I hadn't been to Korea for over twenty years when I first met then-Korean President Park Geun-hye (2013–2017), the first woman president seeking Korean American entrepreneurs in the U.S. for Korea's Innovation Economy initiative. She had appointed me as a member of the Oversight Committee for South Korea's Three-Year Plan for Economic Innovation. During that time, I made frequent visits to Korea for meetings.

On one of those trips, I visited Yeoncheon. We were able to find our old caretaker's son, Mr. Wang. He now manages the farm since the South Korean government has allowed limited access to farming.

"Can I see my grandfather's grave?" I asked.

It was early twilight, but he eagerly agreed and drove us to the bottom of a hill in his Jeep. We climbed up the steep mountain to where my grandfather's gravesite was. Unfortunately, no remnants of tombstones or burial mounds were left—just a little clearing of the flat earth.

Figure 4. Mr Wang, our old caretaker's son, at the site of my grandparent's graves

"How do you know this is the site?" I asked him.

"My dad used to take me here, and we planted these trees together. My father used to take care of your grandfather's grave," he said, pointing to the tall, grown trees around the gravesites.

"My father has been dead for quite some time," Mr. Wang told us. I was sorry to hear this sad news. If he had still lived, he would have remembered me.

After all, our old caretaker and tenant farmer had tended to my grandfather's grave for all these years. To think of Mr. Wang and his father's love and loyalty toward our family, who had been gone for so long now, brought a lump to my throat. So, I marked the grave's location with my iPhone's GPS to come back again.

I looked around, trying to remember the place I knew. Several farmhouses were scattered around the village, but none with thatched roofs anymore—they had been replaced with tin. It was early December 2013, and light snow covered the ground. The surrounding mountains were beautiful and peaceful, and the farm below was quiet and empty of crops. Much later, my older brother, Kigap, said, "You were Harabeoji's (grandfather's) favorite," but I don't remember him much when he was alive. However, when I looked around that landscape, the peaceful hills full of good feng shui, I felt him close to me.

Figure 5. My grandparent's gravesite at Yeoncheon, 2013

MY UNCLE KIM HEE BAEK

My uncle, Kim Hee Baek, was born on October 17, 1899, in Daedong, Pyongan Nam-do, Korea, near Pyongyang (now the Capital of North Korea) and died in November 1937 in Manchuria. He was my mother's oldest brother by fifteen years.

Growing up, my mother repeatedly told us about him, a Korean Freedom Fighter, and her family's sacrifice to support the independence movement. This story was compiled from excerpts from the official Korean government archives and my mother Kim Hee Joo's memoir and her stories.

Japan occupied Korea from 1910 to 1945. Korean resistance began almost immediately but was brutally repressed by the occupying Japanese army. Then, in January 1919, U.S. President Woodrow Wilson outlined the right of self-determination at the World War I Paris Peace Conference. A former emperor of Korea was assassinated by Japanese agents that same month. A few weeks later, on March 1, 1919, thirty-three Korean activists read their Korean Declaration of Independence and sent it to the Japanese Governor-General. The March 1st Movement set in motion the Korean fight for independence.

My uncle attended Yonhui College in Seoul (now Yonsei University, initially founded by an American missionary). He immediately quit school and was among the first to join the movement known as the Korean Independent Army, later the National Organization of Freedom Fighters. My uncle's earliest contributions to the cause of independence were his revolutionary writings that helped stir the people of Korea to fight against the Japanese. Later, he became the 15th president of the organization.

The Japanese army eventually learned about my uncle's activities and targeted him. As a result, he fled from his hometown, Daedong, to Manchuria, where many Korean freedom fighters were in exile. According to my mother's memoir, to avoid the Japanese police, her entire family, including her grandparents, left Pyongyang. They trekked through the mountains to join my uncle in Manchuria on foot. The family left everything behind: their home, my grandfather's business, and the mill to escape the brutal Japanese crackdown and their search for freedom fighters. The journey on foot to Manchuria took the family months of looking for a safe place to settle. They finally arrived in Yongjeong, North Gando, Manchuria. At that time, my mother was only five years old.

My great-grandfather and grandfather on my mother's side became among the first Koreans converted to Christianity by missionaries in the late 1800s. They became devout Christians when less than 1 percent of Koreans were Christians. Upon arrival in Yongjeong, my grandfather established a church, Eunjin Middle School, and Myeongshin Girls' Middle School to educate his daughters and focus on education.

My uncle was one of the most prominent freedom fighters of that era. He was most credited for his fundraising efforts to purchase World War I rifles and other weapons from Czechoslovakia and transporting the weapons to the resistance in various places. He often risked his life to go back and forth from Manchuria to Korea to raise funds to buy these weapons. In addition, he engaged in vigorous armed activities by spying on and sabotaging secret Japanese military operations in the Yeongil district, resulting in many Japanese casualties.

As reported by the Dong-a Ilbo newspaper at the time, after more than five years as a leader of the Korean freedom fighters, he was arrested in the fall of 1924 by the police of the Japanese consulate in Yongjeong (Manchuria). They sent him to Chongjin, where the Chongjin District Court sentenced him to a two-year prison term on January 25, 1925. But, when the Gyeongseong (now Seoul) Criminal Court got word of my uncle's arrest, a big fish, he was ordered to be transferred to Gyeongseong (Seoul) Criminal Court. Finally, on March 16, 1925, he was indicted for alleged robbery and murder. He received a twelve-year sentence and was imprisoned in Seoul's West Gate Maximum Security Prison.

After serving five years and three months, the Japanese released him on the condition that he would not get involved again in the fight for independence. He had contracted tuberculosis in prison and was dying at age thirty-one.

After his release from prison, my uncle returned to Manchuria and rejoined the resistance. He was an intellectual. Despite the warning, he wrote many inspiring articles and pamphlets for the resistance. In November 1937, he died at the age of thirty-eight from malnutrition and tuberculosis.

Kim Hee Baek didn't live to see Korea's independence from Japanese rule on August 15, 1945.

In his will, my uncle wanted to be buried in his ancestors' burial ground in Daedong, Korea, on Independence Day. However, he was buried in the First Church Cemetery in Myeongwol-gu, Manchuria. His family could never carry out his last wish because of the division of Korea into South and North after liberation.

In 1977, to honor my uncle's heroic deeds for Korean independence, the government of South Korea posthumously awarded him the National Order of Founding Fathers of Independence (equivalent to the U.S. Medal of Honor), and in 1990, he was awarded the National Order of Patriotism (equivalent to the U.S. Medal of Freedom).

Figure 6. The South Korean government's Official Registry of my uncle Kim Hee Baek

I realized how much I had inherited my uncle's spirit of patriotism, even for my adopted country of America.

If Korea is ever united and I am still living, I would like to find my uncle's grave in Manchuria and bring his remains to his hometown, as he desired in his will.

MY FATHER

The college entrance exam was seen as the most crucial thing in determining your future in Korea, as it still is now. I attended Hakwon, an after-school class in high school, to prepare for the college entrance exam. And I came home late at night by bus.

The nearest bus stop was in front of the university, a mile away. After getting off, I had to walk through a narrow street between two campuses, usually deserted at night. I got off the bus around 10 o'clock every night with a few other people, each of whom went in a different direction.

My father used to wait for me at the bus stop, and we walked home together. It was one of my fondest memories of my father. He loved his children and worried about my coming home late at night. He was unlike many other typical Korean fathers at that time who often stayed out late after work, drinking with their buddies. He was a devout Christian and never drank or smoked.

I've always claimed that I was my father's favorite child, and he often said I was the smartest, too! He used to take me to the construction sites he worked on even though I was a girl and the middle child of his six children.

When I graduated first from my class at the most prestigious university in Korea, my parents were so proud—they had great expectations for me.

However, when I was accepted to graduate school in America, my father worried that I would be educated too much, miss the opportunity to be married, and live my entire life as an old maid.

"Don't worry, Dad. I will get my PhD, return to Korea, and be a professor," I assured him confidently.

"Even if you return, no man will marry a highly educated old woman." So he argued, feeling sad about sending his daughter so far away.

I promised I would return, "coming home in a golden robe," as the old Korean saying goes.

~~~

As a young man, my father moved from Kyung-sang Nam-do, a southern province of Korea, to Manchuria with his family. During the Japanese occupation and colonization, he spent his youth attending schools in Manchuria, which were run by missionaries. In his early years in the 1930s and 1940s, my father became successful in the construction business in Manchuria.

He had many Japanese clients and used to say, "There are good Japanese, too."

One of his Japanese clients told him that the war would soon be over and that he should consider moving to Seoul.

My father had, in fact, always dreamed of eventually settling in Seoul. So, with this new information from his client, he moved his family from Manchuria to Seoul before Korea's liberation on August 15, 1945.

When he arrived in the city, he got into several business deals but soon found it difficult to adjust and establish a new life without his old business network. He lost money quickly.

Figure 7. Lumber yard in Manchuria, my father 2nd from the left with his employees

"He was too honest and trusted people too much!" my mother used to say. People who knew him also said that he was naturally honest. The hardships of the long years of Japanese colonization and the wars had hardened the Korean people. Gentle people like my father, who was not tough enough, couldn't survive. He never fully recovered his business acumen or confidence.

He became desperate with a young family and his parents to care for. With the last of his remaining money, he bought our farm. Father died several years after I came to America, and I never saw him again. He was a defeated man who lost his fortune to his fellow citizens and lost his farm in the Korean War. But he never blamed God for his misfortunes. He was always proud of his children and loved his family.

When I got the news that my father had died of a massive stroke, I was having a difficult pregnancy, which precluded me from traveling. In any case, I didn't have the money to return to Korea. Seeing the pictures of his funeral that my sister sent me later, my heart ached, and I missed him so much.

I wondered if he would have had a better chance in America, a Land of Opportunity, where hard work gets rewarded, and his honesty and integrity would have been better valued. He might have enjoyed the stability of life and fortune without the constant wars.

I wish he lived long enough to come and see our lives and successes here in America. He always busied himself fixing things around the house. He never sat around except when he was playing his favorite chess games. Whenever I saw something needing repair in the house, I used to say, "Oh, my father could have fixed this if he were here." He would have enjoyed that and loved helping the kids, too. Whenever my sister and I share a watermelon, his favorite fruit, we often talk about how much Dad would have enjoyed American watermelon, which is bigger and sweeter.

My father taught me many lifelong lessons about the importance of an authentic and loving family.

Years later, when I returned to Korea, I visited his cemetery for the first time. My father was buried in a public Christian cemetery not far south of Yeoncheon, where my grandfather was buried. Unfortunately, at my father's death, it was not accessible to the public.

Many years after he died, I had a recurring dream about my father. The dream felt so real. In it, he was kind, gentle, and waiting for me, just like he always had been. But he was always in the distance, and I could never touch him.

COMING TO AMERICA

It was a clear early summer day in June 1966. I climbed the stairs and boarded an Air Canada jet, waving goodbye at the Gimpo Airport outside Seoul. I was leaving Korea, the first in my family to go and study in America.

My whole family—my parents, brothers, and sisters—came to the airport. In addition, several close friends and even my cousins came to wish me safe travels.

I wore a new, custom-tailored, stylish, pink eyelet suit in size two. It had a tight skirt, a short-sleeve jacket, and a white chiffon V-neck collar. I had saved the money and went to a dressmaker in Myung Dong, Seoul's fashion

Figure 8. My passport photo, 1966

district, for this special occasion suit. I had a short haircut like Audrey Hepburn, which was fashionable then.

Everyone was sad on the tarmac, and my mom was crying. Mother lived in Seoul and separated from her family in the North when Korea was divided into North and South after World War II in 1945. She never saw them again. She always missed and longed for her younger sister.

This time, her daughter was leaving. We thought we would never see each other again once I left. Korea was one of the poorest countries in the world after the Korean War, and jet air travel was new and expensive.

However, the excitement of going to the new world and the great expectations for the future took over the sadness of parting. Perhaps leaving was easier than being left behind.

Upon graduating from Seoul National University, I worked two jobs while preparing my applications to graduate schools in America. During the day, I worked as a ticketing agent dealing primarily with foreigners at the Korea Travel Bureau, a government agency. In addition, I taught geography in evening classes at a girls' high school in Seoul for about a year. The Korea Travel Bureau arranged free airplane tickets from Seoul to Philadelphia, which would have cost me a fortune.

When I announced that I was accepted to a graduate school in America, my parents had many discussions about what to do with me. My father was hesitant, but my mother was rather brave, saying, "She has a great opportunity. We should let her go." She won the debate. But it didn't matter. I was determined to go anyway.

Going to America to study was still rare, especially for a young woman. It was limited to the children of elite and wealthy families. My family was neither, but I was an accomplished student graduating from the prestigious Seoul National University at the top of my class. In addition, I received a full scholarship from Clark University in Massachusetts, internationally known for its Graduate School of Geography, which made my journey to America possible.

I aimed to get my PhD, return to Korea to my alma mater, and teach geography. I was a protégé and had pretty good assurance from my professor, the department's chair, Professor Yuk. "Please come back as soon as you finish your PhD. We will have a seat for you," he said with a kind smile when I went to see him to say goodbye.

~~~

I flew many hours across the Pacific. Finally, I woke up early in the morning, and the first thing I saw from the airplane window was Victoria, Canada. The scenery was picture perfect: white houses with red tile roofs dotted the rocky coastline; so beautiful—just like how I imagined America would be. I had arrived in the New World!

It took about twenty-eight hours to fly from Seoul to Philadelphia, stopping at Seattle airport, where I changed planes to United Airlines.

Seattle airport, the first place I landed in the U.S., was newly renovated, a big and impressive building with floor-to-ceiling glass walls, almost thirty feet tall, but it wasn't crowded, unlike Gimpo Airport. I was awed like a country girl looking around, even though I grew up in a big city.

Then, finally, I caught a glimpse of America! I waited a couple of hours to change the flight. People were curious about a young Asian woman traveling alone and stopped to ask if I needed any help, where I was going, or where I was from, and some asked if I was Japanese. *Do I dress like I'm Japanese, or do they think all Asians are Japanese?* But they all seemed to be friendly and genuinely trying to help.

I was carrying a big suitcase with all my possessions. I carefully packed two wool suits—gray and brown—several dresses, and a new black winter coat. I also packed two Korean costumes for special occasions: a pink embroidered satin dress for winter, a farewell gift from my friend's sister, and another pink silk dress for summer, a gift from my best friend's mother, all custom-made. Also, an English-Korean dictionary, a couple of textbooks, and several gift items in the bag: silk ties and lacquer cigarette boxes for the professors or other people I would meet, a part of Korean customs.

Around midnight, I landed in Philadelphia, my first destination, where my Korean sponsor family lived. The wife, Agnes, was my friend's sister, and they were happy to have me for the summer. I came early to polish my English and earn some money before going to school, and I stayed with them until school started in September. All the passengers met with families and friends and disappeared, but I could not find my sponsor. It was pitch dark outside and quiet. I became worried and scared—stranded at this strange airport in the dead of night, knowing no one.

I finally found a public telephone booth and tried to call my sponsor, but the operator kept saying, "insert a dime." I didn't understand what a "dime" was. Finally, I hailed someone to help me. Luckily, a young woman came up and put 10 cents of her own money in for me. I was so thankful for her kindness. It was my first lesson in American English because there was so much about American English that I couldn't have known from textbooks.

A groggy voice answered the phone as if waking up, "Oh, we thought you were arriving at noontime tomorrow. Just wait there. We will be there within half an hour." Somehow, there was confusion about a.m. and p.m. I was relieved to be rescued.

My sponsor family, the Kims, James and Agnes, lived with their toddler son and daughter in a new garden apartment complex, a group of three-story brick buildings in King of Prussia, a suburb of Philadelphia.

"One of the first garden apartments in the area. Most of our friends still live in the old tenement houses in the city," they told me proudly.

They arranged a room for me, moving their one-year-old son to their bedroom in a crib, and I shared the second bedroom with their three-year-old daughter. Finally, after so many hours of flight, I fell asleep like a baby.

The complex had a big community swimming pool with a clubhouse and a small convenience store, where many young, educated professional families lived. My sponsor family was one of those typical families. Mr. James Kim had a PhD in economics from the Wharton School and taught at nearby Villanova University. With a master's degree in home economics from Peabody College, Agnes—my friend's sister—cared for their two toddlers at home. James and Agnes loved playing bridge and other card games and often went to the clubhouse to play in the evenings while I babysat their children.

There was a picture on the mantle of Agnes where she wore a long white gown like a wedding dress and her escort in a tux. She looked beautiful with her long, curly brown hair, big brown eyes, and slim figure.

I asked about the picture, and she laughed, "I was a Homecoming Queen at Peabody. My father thought I was getting married to an American guy and was so upset."

The following day, I ventured outside. Even though it was early morning, the hot and humid air engulfed me, mixed with the smell of fresh-cut grass. This impression and the air lingered in me for many years. Whenever I smell fresh-cut grass on hot summer days, it reminds me of that first summer in America.

In front of the apartment building, the vast rolling greens sloped toward the single-story brick building that housed the convenience store. I sat down on a grassy knoll and breathed deeply—like breathing in the new surroundings.

I grew up in a city where the houses were so compact that you could talk to your neighbors over the fence. The sprawling green lawns and vast open space made me feel like I was in a park.

Less than forty-eight hours earlier, I left Korea and was now in America. I had finally arrived in the New World! My new life had begun.

SUMMER OF 1966

Upon my arrival in Philadelphia, Agnes put this note on her club's bulletin board. I had been a high school teacher in Korea, and I would have never thought of doing odd jobs there—it would have been considered degrading. However, I came early to polish my English and make money to survive.

> ## HELP AVAILABLE:
>
> *Young female graduate student looking for summer jobs, babysitting, mother's helper, and household chores.*

The first call was to babysit a newborn, a baby boy, a few months old. When I arrived, I immediately heard the familiar sound of classical music. I felt at home and told the baby's parents I loved this music.

"We will leave it on then so that you can listen," Dr. Myers responded happily. They were all dressed up; Dr. Myers in a suit and tie and Mrs. Myers in a beautiful flowery, pale pink dress, ready for dinner. Mrs. Myers ushered me down the hall to the baby's room.

"He is ready to sleep, but please check on him occasionally. We won't be too long, maybe a couple of hours,"

Mrs. Myers said, closing the door quietly. The baby was awake, and his eyes fixed on the Merry-Go-Round animal musical toy set on the crib.

Once they left, I frequently tiptoed into the baby's room to ensure he was okay until he fell asleep. Then I sat in the living room and listened to music. Sibelius's violin concerto was one of my favorite pieces of music. Again, I felt overcome by homesickness—thinking of my family and friends whom I left behind. Tears swelled up, and I couldn't control myself shamelessly crying.

Even though I calmed down when the Myers came home, they must have sensed something and asked, looking at me seriously, "Was everything alright?" I quickly said everything was fine, took the money, and left hurriedly.

The word got around that I was looking for work, and another woman in the neighborhood, Mrs. Myers's classmate at Smith College, called me about an ironing job. She also had a newborn but set up the ironing board in the kitchen for me with several men's shirts, her blouses, and bedsheets to iron. She was working in the kitchen while I was ironing and asked several questions: Where am I going to school, what will I major in, and whether I have a place to stay when I get to school? I told her I would be looking for an apartment but didn't have any place to stay. She suggested I should inquire at the YWCA dormitory in Worcester. I thanked her and said I'd keep it in mind.

My third job was for the middle-aged woman upstairs.

"My spring cleaning is way behind. First, we need to clean the windows, just inside, and woodwork," she said. I didn't know what cleaning "woodwork" was but soon discovered it entailed washing the moldings, door, and window frames. The windows had thin plastic louver shutters, and I accidentally cut my finger while cleaning them. It was sharp as a knife. My finger was bleeding badly, and I asked for a Band-Aid. I must have screamed. Her son came out of nowhere, wiped the blood off, and put the Band-Aid on my finger, gently holding my hand. He was about my age, and I felt embarrassed about my arm being touched by an American man. Maybe he thought it, too, because his face was flushed red when I looked at him.

The last job was a big one—living with three teenage girls for a week in Ardmore, the Main Line section of Philadelphia. I don't remember how I got the job outside of the apartment complex where I was staying. However, the beautiful, rambling single-story house sat on the manicured ground in an impressive neighborhood surrounded by mansions.

My job was to ensure the girls behaved while their proud parents, a handsome couple in their mid-forties, took their oldest son on a New England college tour. They mentioned "Harvard" among the several schools to be touring, and they took off.

The girls were self-sufficient: helping themselves with meals, cold cereals and orange juice for breakfast, and making tuna fish sandwiches for lunch—*these American sandwiches are delicious*—I thought. Korean breakfast was usually a big main meal, and we never had cereals for breakfast. Instead, in Korea, we ate cereals—wheat, barley, rice, and corn—as a snack, like popcorn. And we didn't have milk at home either. The girls were lovely—the youngest, about thirteen, skinny and mild-mannered; the older one, about fifteen or sixteen, clearly in charge of her younger sisters; and one in the middle. Even the younger one was almost my height. I learned from the girls that their father owned a printing company, and their brother would be a senior in a private high school. He was an excellent student, getting straight As. They all seemed to be proud of their brother.

The week went by fast, and the parents were happy when they returned with no incidents to report. I was paid more than the sum I earned from my previous jobs. I learned a lot living with an American family for the first time, how these children in their teens were so independent, could entertain themselves, and were casual in interacting with me, not shy.

I was shocked when they called me by my first name. In Korea, that would be unheard of! We call any older person by their last name or profession, like "teacher" or "doctor," as a sign of respect. Even between siblings, you never call an older sibling by their name. Instead, we refer to them as 'sister" or "brother." Even though the children were very respectful, it was a big cultural difference I wasn't accustomed to!

Besides babysitting, cleaning, and ironing, I had another experience during that summer. A young woman—perhaps in her late twenties—lived above the Kims' apartment. She was from Hong Kong, had a master's degree in art history, and owned a Chinese restaurant. She was also strikingly tall, towering over me at almost six feet in her traditional tight Chinese dress and high heels.

She had asked Agnes, who was my guardian, if I would like to do some waitressing.

I had heard that waitressing made the most money for a summer job because of good tips, and I was excited to begin.

The restaurant was in Conshohocken, Pennsylvania, an industrial town, and I had to take a train from King of Prussia, outside Philadelphia, where I lived. They also informed me that I had to wear a uniform: a black skirt and white blouse that Agnes hurriedly procured.

I often reflect on how kind Agnes was to me during this time. She was like an older sister; she taught me how to make dresses, hustled to get me jobs, and was always concerned that I had enough to eat.

It wasn't a big restaurant, with about twenty tables of two or four seats. The interior was dark and long, without windows and only several dim, low-hanging ceiling lights.

When I entered the restaurant, a middle-aged white waitress walked straight to the door and said, without any greetings, "Come, follow me. I will show you around."

She was a short, stout woman in her mid to late forties and wore the same black and white uniform as mine, with ear-length graying hair. I learned her name was Martha, and she seemed to be the only waitress working there and was in charge of training me. First, she showed me where the tea and table settings were.

Martha must have been waitressing for a long time, being efficient and knowing what she was doing. But she was like a drill sergeant. She wasn't friendly, never smiled, and ensured I understood she was the boss.

"Just these last two tables for you," she said, pointing at two tables near the door.

"If Black people come in, have them sit at those tables. Oh, and by the way, don't serve them tea unless they ask."

That gave me a powerful impression. But, of course, Korea, at that time, was very homogeneous, so there weren't any racial issues.

On my first day, in the evening, a young Black man came in alone for dinner. I led him to one of those designated tables. I felt terrible, but I didn't dare do otherwise. However, I served him tea even though he didn't ask; it was the least I could do.

I was eager to work hard, so I greeted everyone who walked in and led them to a table. When I welcomed the customer to a table designated for the other waitress, I didn't intend to take the table from her—I just wanted to ensure that the customers got our attention. Therefore, the customers were nice to me and engaged in conversation. But she thought I was intruding on her territory. She considered me either a threat to her or insubordinate. Then, she asked the owner to fire me. I was let go in a couple of days. So, my waitressing job ended almost as soon as it had begun!

However, my very short time as a waitress was not in vain. Before being fired, I met a woman named Kevin Geuther. She walked in with two adopted Korean girls, ages two and three. She was surprised to see a young Korean student waiting at tables at her regular lunch spot and excited to talk about her two daughters, Gina and Kim, from Korea. Gina's skin was much lighter than Kim's, and she was very shy. We talked for a while, and I learned the girls had been in this country only a few months, were quiet, and didn't seem to understand English. So, I said to them in Korean

"You are pretty," to see their reactions. Gina's eyes were wide open in surprise, but she didn't respond. However, I knew she recognized the language. I felt sorry for the girls who were orphans, but at the same time, I was happy they would be better cared for in America.

Kevin was in her thirties, had blue eyes and shoulder-length blond hair, and seemed to genuinely love her adopted daughters. International adoptions were unusual then, but American families started adopting orphans from Korea after the war. Kevin was so happy to have a cultural connection with her children that she invited me to her house. I felt at ease around Kevin and her two children and accepted her invitation. She asked me where I lived and said she would come and pick me up.

The following day, she came to the apartment. Agnes came out to greet her. Looking at Kevin's big, impressive white car, her eyes widened in astonishment. Agnes whispered to me in Korean, "That's a Lincoln Continental! My dream car and it's expensive!"

They introduced themselves, and Kevin asked Agnes if it was okay for me to stay overnight. I assumed it would be only a day visit, unprepared for an overnight trip, and hurriedly went in to pack an overnight bag with Agnes's consent. Soon, we drove off in the Lincoln Continental! I had no idea what kind of car that was. My dream at that time was to own a Volkswagen Beetle.

After a long drive outside the city, we arrived at Kevin's house in Lansdale, Pennsylvania. A big, round brass gong was on the door with a drumstick hanging at the side.

She took the drumstick, banged the gong, and said laughing, "This is my doorbell."

The single-story house looked new, surrounded by a wide-open field. Upon entering, I instantly liked the open, contemporary design with a white grand piano in the center of the living room and a round, white leather sofa in front of the fireplace, like in a hotel lobby. They even had a color television! It was the first time I had seen one. I thought, *in the future, I want to build a house like this!*

The only problem was that they had two Dobermans. They looked menacing. I'd never seen a Doberman in Korea, but Kevin calmed me down, saying they were harmless, and took them to the fenced-in backyard through the big, wide sliding door.

Later, she said, "I've planned a surprise for you."

I didn't understand what she meant by "surprise," but I went along. She took me to a hair salon and had my hair shampooed, cut, and styled. Of course, she had her hair done, too. But then I realized I hadn't had my haircut since I left Korea a few months ago. I must have looked like I needed a haircut badly!

In the evening, her husband, Gene, came home. He was a pilot and seemed a lot older than Kevin. He was warm and welcoming.

"You know, our names are switched. Kevin has a man's name, and I have a woman's. And people get confused," he said, smiling. I didn't know much about American men's and women's names, except the obvious ones like John and Mary, so it hadn't struck me as odd! But many years later, I named my son Kevin!

Kevin must have planned and discussed the day with Gene. In the evening, they took me to dinner without their children. They must have gotten a babysitter—I don't remember that detail. First, we sat at the bar. They had been regular customers by the way the bartender greeted them.

"What kind of cocktail would you like?" the bartender asked me.

My father never drank, and there was no alcohol in our house, so I had no idea. The only alcoholic drink I'd ever had was a glass of beer at my college graduation day celebration in Seoul. In my short dress, I might have looked like a teenager, but the bartender never questioned my age in the company of the Geuthers.

They looked at my bewildered face, and Gene said, "I will order one for you. You will like it."

He called the bartender, "Tom Collins for her."

The drink came in a tall, skinny, frosted glass, slightly yellowish. I sipped slowly. It was sweet and delicious, so I drank a little faster. Kevin enjoyed just watching me and said, "You should slow down. It has alcohol in it." Soon, I felt the buzz and realized it wasn't just fruit juice.

After that, if people asked me for a cocktail, I said, "Tom Collins, please." It was the only drink I knew, then.

The following year, on my first Easter in America, Kevin invited me to come and stay with them. I got a ride from a female graduate student in the chemistry department who lived near Landsdale and spent Easter with Kevin and Gene. We became good friends. Kevin packed a lovely picnic basket of ham sandwiches for our drive back to school.

I kept in touch with Kevin for several years, but that was the last time I saw them. She was my first American friend and very nice to me. After that, however, I lost touch with Kevin and the girls, but still thought about them often and wondered what happened to them.

That summer was an intensive cultural immersion for me! Every experience was heightened. I remember the contrasts between my culture and this new one were starkly distinguished in those first few months. There was so much to learn, but I loved it as I was eager to throw myself into American culture; plus, I made some money, too! Because of that experience, I was more comfortable in that new environment when I went to school that fall. It could have been a considerable culture shock otherwise.

CULTURE SHOCK

It was a turbulent time in America when I first arrived in the U.S. The 1960s saw significant societal changes: civil rights marches led by Martin Luther King, Jr., riots in most cities, and anti-Vietnam War demonstrations on university campuses. It was an unsettling and hostile environment, especially for newcomers like me.

Then, in early August in Philadelphia, the Kims, and I were glued to the television—there had been a mass shooting at the University of Texas in Austin.

It was a hot summer morning, and the gunman started shooting from the top of the University of Texas Tower. He fired randomly at pedestrians below. While the killing spree continued, hundreds of students and professors ran for cover, crouched behind trees and anywhere they could hide in an otherwise quiet campus. Later, television showed students hiding under desks and beds, playing dead. It was horrific, even evil.

Soon, I would be going to university, and I was scared that this rampage was happening at a university campus. I'd never seen such violence and never found out what triggered the person, allegedly a student, to commit such a heinous crime. It had an incredible impact on me, and sadly, it is still happening today.

Coming from Korea then, I'd never even heard of or considered something like this. Of course I'd lived through the war, but this was peacetime—I couldn't fathom or grasp something like this. During the war, we were under our parents' protection as children. I came here alone and felt so vulnerable. Nobody was protecting me, and that perhaps was a difference too.

Shortly after that, in early 1967, I lived alone in an apartment near the campus at Clark University in Worcester, Massachusetts, when there was a statewide manhunt for the "Boston Strangler," who had escaped from Bridgewater State Hospital.

I didn't have a television but listened to the details of his crime on the radio about how he entered apartments of unsuspecting women, raped, and strangled them with their stockings—hence the name "Boston Strangler"—and killed many single women of all ages. The radio warned people, especially single women like me, to lock their doors and not let anybody in. Even in broad daylight, I was too scared to go outside. Luckily, the Strangler was captured quickly, and I could free myself from lockdown.

On top of that, on campus at Clark, there were frequent anti-Vietnam war demonstrations. The height of the violent protests happened in the summer of 1967 when Vice President Hubert Humphrey came to Clark University for the opening of the Goddard Library, named after Robert H. Goddard, the father of modern rocket propulsion and who had received his PhD in Physics from Clark University. Many student demonstrators were injured and arrested by the police.

What kind of country is this? There was so much violence, I thought. I jumped into this environment soon after arriving in the U.S. I never told my parents what was happening, as they would have been distraught.

During that long, hot summer of 1967, riots burned cities across the country, especially in Detroit, Baltimore, Newark, and Plainfield, New Jersey—captured on the cover of Time Magazine. The riots mainly stemmed from racial injustice—cities were burning, and the marches continued, but there seemed to be no solutions to the problems. We still have so much work to do in this area—over fifty years since I first witnessed the riots.

In the late 1960s and early 1970s, the American feminist movement came—the women's liberation movement. A diverse social movement, primarily based in the United States, sought equal rights and opportunities and greater personal freedom for women.

The Civil Rights Act of 1964 prohibited discrimination based on race, religion, color, or national origin in public places, schools, and employment. Discrimination based on sex was not initially included. As a result, the National Organization for Women (NOW) was formed in October 1966. And, to many people's disappointment, the Equal Employment Opportunity Commission (EEOC) did not seem willing or able to carry out that part of the law's mandate.

I was shocked to learn that American women could not have checkbooks or credit cards without their father or husband cosigning. But, on the other hand, in Korea, many women ran the household and its finances like matriarchs, especially those living in cities, even though most women would not work outside the home.

On arriving in the U.S., I perceived that women were treated respectfully, opening car doors and putting ladies first, like "Ladies and Gentlemen." In Korea, it would be addressed as "Gentlemen and Ladies." But this was perhaps not the case when you scratched the surface, and they had no agency outside their husbands.

After the Korean War, my mother started selling and trading rice grains. There were food shortages, primarily rice, the staple of the Korean diet, and the government rationed long-grain rice from international food aid to families. Moreover, Koreans were not accustomed to long-grain and preferred short-grain rice. Some affluent families wanted to exchange long-grain with short-grain rice, even at a higher price. My mother saw the opportunity and jumped into business by buying, selling, and trading rice and other grains.

She had no previous business experience but learned to run the business independently and helped the family.

I also learned to compete with men at a male-dominated Seoul National University in Korea and thrived!

MEETING KIM

It was a crisp morning in mid-August 1966, and I was planning to head to school in Massachusetts the next day.

"We'd love to take you! We have a good friend outside of Boston whom we haven't seen for a long time. We'll stop by and see him, so it's no trouble," James said as he poured a morning cup of coffee. It was decided.

And so the next day, James and the rest of my sponsor family in Philadelphia drove me to Massachusetts for the start of the school year, with two little toddlers and me in the back seat of the Kims' new white Mustang. While driving through a long stretch of highway in Connecticut and Massachusetts, Agnes admired the passing woodlands.

"You know, Kija, these trees will be so beautiful in the fall here in New England," she smiled back at me from the passenger seat. Even though it was in the middle of August, there was a hint of fall, and some of the leaves near the lakes were already changing colors.

After hours of driving in the late afternoon, we pulled into the driveway of a small, barn-red ranch house on a somewhat busy road in North Reading. A gray Porsche and a red Volvo were parked on the gravel.

James's friend was home early, anticipating our arrival. The house looked like a typical bachelor pad: scantily furnished with a Scandinavian-style couch, a chair, and a small wooden coffee table with no rug in the living room.

It was not messy, but not tidy either. We were to stay there for a few days before continuing to my school.

James introduced his friend, Kim, as an old high school buddy, and I said *Anyunghaseiyo*, a hello in Korean, and politely moved away. They were busy catching up and talking excitedly in Korean. Kim seemed quiet but not unfriendly. I didn't remember, but he later told me I wore a yellow mini-dress. I remembered that dress—Agnes had helped me make it over the summer.

A chubby American guy, his roommate in his mid-twenties, was in and out in his Porsche all day long. The visit to North Reading was, on the whole, uneventful. My most vivid memory from that visit was getting sick the first night after eating dinner at a Chinese restaurant. They were all worried. I must have been tired and carsick after the long drive. I was so self-conscious and embarrassed about such trouble—I felt it was not a good first impression as a guest.

I was also struck by just how cold it was in New England. I felt a vulnerability in this new environment that I hadn't felt in Philadelphia in the safety of my host family's home. The cold only seemed to highlight this feeling of being alone. Even now sometimes, when the season turns into fall, I remember that time and how melancholy I felt.

My first impression of Worcester, where Clark University is located, was that it was disappointingly old and small! There were no high rises and only a few department stores downtown. I also spotted several funeral homes—too many for the town's size! Even the campus didn't look like it did in the brochure and was very small compared to Seoul National University.

After the campus tour, I was dropped off at the YWCA dormitory, an old brick building downtown, where I would stay until I found an apartment. I checked in, dragged my luggage to my room on the second floor, and met several other young women staying there.

Suddenly, I was by myself and couldn't overcome my loneliness. I missed home, family, and friends in Korea; the family dinnertime when everybody sat around and shared the day's stories; listening to classical music in the tearoom with friends for hours—Beethoven, Mozart, Tchaikovsky, Sibelius, and Rachmaninoff—if you stayed long enough, you could hear the same piece more than once. I never got tired of listening to the music. I sat on my bed in the dorm and stared at the blank wall and wondered if I'd ever feel that sense of belonging here in America.

In early September, school started. I met my professors and classmates. Five international students, including me, were among about twenty graduate students: a couple from Sri Lanka, one from Taiwan, and another from England—all male students except the wife from Sri Lanka and me. I began settling into the school routine.

However, I still couldn't find an apartment. Each time I followed a newspaper ad, I was too late. So, I went to the school counselor's office for help. Fortunately, they introduced me to a lovely family with three little boys—a baby and two toddlers—looking for a live-in nanny to help babysit the boys occasionally in the evening in exchange for room and board. It was in West Boylston, just outside Worcester, but there was a bus line to the school. So, I took it, moving out of the YWCA dormitory. The husband was the school district's new superintendent, and there were frequent night meetings. However, the arrangement was good because I could study at night in my room and live with a family.

Then, in early October, I had an unexpected visitor at school. I didn't remember his name, but I recognized him: James's friend from North Reading. I was quite surprised but courteous. He suggested driving out to a nearby lake, where, he said, the foliage was spectacular in the fall.

We sat on a park bench, and the autumn leaves reflected in the water in all their brilliant reds and burnt oranges.

We talked pleasantly and shared stories, mostly he asked questions first: what schools I went to, where I lived in Seoul. He came to America right after Kyung-Gi High School, the most prestigious boys' high school in Seoul, and went to Worcester Polytechnic Institute (WPI) in Worcester. He was an engineer at a semiconductor company near Boston, an emerging technology company. He had been in the U.S. for almost ten years. His name was Simyung Kim, but Americans called him "Kim."

When I mentioned I went to Sook-Myung Girls' High School in Seoul, he said, surprised, "I had a cousin who went there. Do you know Sohee Lee?"

"I know her well. We were classmates. She lived nearby, and I used to stop by her house in the morning, and we went to school together. However, often she wasn't ready, and we were tardy to school because of her." I knew her family well and discovered her mother and Kim's mother were sisters.

Furthermore, at one point, Kim and I lived in the same town in Seoul. I even knew his house, not far from my home. I remembered that James once mentioned his friend (Kim) in North Reading was from a prominent family in Korea. What a small world!

The Korean student community was tiny then, and there was a joke among us, "If you don't find any mutual friends and families in ten minutes of talk, then the person is probably a North Korean spy."

Soon, Kim made more frequent visits. Since he was James's classmate, I guessed he was around thirty— about six years older than me. He seemed much more established than me, a student and a newcomer. He had an excellent job as an engineer, had been in America a long time, had many Korean friends, and knew his way around the city. However, I was worried and conflicted about his frequent visits, taking my time away from studying.

I once mentioned my difficulties finding an apartment at the start of the school year and that I'd had no luck. He volunteered to find a place for me, and he did. I was thankful for his help in the things that felt so overwhelming. In addition, he was my close friend's cousin, and knowing his family made me feel at ease. And I gradually looked forward to his visits during this emotionally uncertain time of loneliness.

When I was lonely, sometimes extremely lonely, I regretted coming to America and wondered, *What if I had stayed in Korea? I would have friends, a better social life, be close to my family, and be in my culture.* The relationship with Kim gave me a small connection to this feeling of home and made things bearable.

And so it took me by great surprise when, one day, he announced out of the blue that he had accepted a new job and was moving to Indianapolis. Excitedly, he also said he was looking for a house there to buy. I was confused about what would happen to our relationship, but he seemed confident it would work out.

He moved before Christmas and invited me to come and visit. However, he still had some unfinished business and often came to Boston. Whenever he arrived, he stayed with me in my apartment. We started discussing our future together, and he suggested I transfer to Indiana University.

During the Christmas holiday, he visited Korea to see his parents. I was eager to hear how the visit went because he'd implied that he would get his parents' blessing so we could get married. But when he returned, his demeanor changed, and he was almost mean to me. His parents had vehemently opposed our getting married. They said my family was not up to par socially and economically with them. So, his parents would arrange for a woman in Korea for him to marry. He had an older brother and two sisters, all married and arranged by their parents, not uncommon in Korea then, and I wasn't surprised. However, I was hurt by the rejection from his parents and the change in his attitude. No one had ever rejected me, and I was angry that my family was humiliated. After that, we stopped communicating, no more phone calls or visits. We were done.

Soon after this, however, I found out that I was pregnant. I was devastated. After weeks of agonizing about what to do, I built up my courage and called him. He didn't believe me, said I was lying, and hung up. I couldn't believe such a betrayal. From then on, I decided to handle the situation by myself. I was ashamed of my poor judgment and behavior in ever getting involved with him in the first place and blamed myself for everything.

After many sleepless nights thinking about what to do, I decided to keep the baby. Abortion was illegal and out of the question. And I didn't want to give the baby up for adoption either. Instead, I could find a church and ask for help—someplace where I could have a baby, look for a job, and raise the baby independently. Then, perhaps, I would disappear, where no one could find me. Returning to Korea was not even the last option—it simply wasn't one. I could not go back in shame. I was alone in this country, still going to school, and didn't have anyone to turn to. I hadn't told anyone and kept all these thoughts to myself.

However, after the final exam in late May, I decided to go to Indiana to look for him.

I lived by then at the "Goddard Home for the Aged" in a big brick Goddard mansion named after Rocket Science's father on Main Street. I worked in the dining hall before and after school hours for my room and board and a little stipend. It was a good arrangement for me to have my room to study and be surrounded by people. I got permission for a weekend off, packed an overnight bag, and bought a roundtrip ticket from New York to Indianapolis. It was a raw, gray day, matching my mood. I took a Greyhound bus from Worcester to New York and flew to Indiana. It was late spring, but New England's weather was still cold, and I had to wear a coat.

I called him at the Indianapolis Airport and waited a long time for him to come out. While waiting, a thought came through my mind that he might not come out after all. Fear and disappointment swept through me. Finally, he arrived in what seemed like a couple of hours later. It was a tough encounter. We sat in the car quietly, staring at the windshield, and he still didn't believe it even though I was almost six months pregnant and quite visible. I would have turned around and returned, but I didn't have enough strength. I persuaded him to let me stay until I had the baby. I stayed with him for twenty more years.

PART TWO

INDIANA 1967 TO 1970

Kenneth

On June 27, 1967, Kenneth was born more than two months premature. He only weighed five pounds but was twenty inches long. I couldn't think straight—everything had happened so fast and unexpectedly. The due date was late August or early September, and I was unprepared.

I was a student and didn't have money or a car to get around to get anything anyway. Therefore, I didn't have any clothes ready or a single piece of furniture apart from the bassinet someone gave me. I was so naive, and it was overwhelming.

When I was rushed to the hospital, the doctors performed a cesarean because he was premature. The baby looked so much like his father when he was born, but the first thing Kim said was *the baby looks just like his cousin.* I was hurt because there was an element of surprise there. As if, up to that point, he hadn't believed the baby was his—like there was no trust.

I had never been to a doctor until I went to Indiana. There was no prenatal care for the baby, and I wondered if that was why he was born so prematurely. When I was discharged a week later, the doctor told his father and me that his lungs were not fully developed, and that we should keep him at the hospital longer. However, we didn't have insurance and asked the doctor if we could take the baby home. He reluctantly agreed and said we had to keep the baby warm. Then, he mentioned President Kennedy lost a premature baby in a similar situation, but I couldn't digest what that meant.

So, we brought the baby home after about a week in the hospital incubator, laying him in the bassinet and keeping him warm, as the doctor said. I checked on him every so often. Then, in the late afternoon, he stopped breathing and died.

I was devastated. A thousand thoughts whirred around my head. *Why did such a sad thing happen to me? Was it God's punishment? What did I do so badly to deserve this? Why didn't he take me with him?* It was too much pain for me to bear.

After the baby died, Kim and I needed each other to endure the sorrow and pain. Even though the relationship didn't start in a healthy way, we stayed together, united in our grief. But we never spoke of Kenneth. He just remained in our thoughts.

Many years later, I asked Kim, "What would have happened to us if I had left there and then?" He responded without emotion or hesitancy, "We would have been just 'old acquaintances.'"

We left Indiana in March 1970 for New Jersey, and I haven't been back there since. There is an unmarked grave of a firstborn baby to an unwed mother under a tree by the cemetery road that I need to visit before I die. Someday, I will make the trip by myself. Only two people, his dad and I, knew of his existence in this world. He lived only about a week. Fifty-four years ago. He was named Kenneth after his father's college roommate, but I never had a chance to call his name.

Kevin

In the fall of 1967, Kim and I married at a county building in Indiana under the auspices of a Justice of the Peace. I wore a light gray dress, almost white, my favorite, that I had brought from Korea. I didn't buy anything special for the wedding, and somehow we didn't have any wedding photos either. A few of Kim's work colleagues came from Boston, including a friendly couple, Jerrie and Paul Witalis, who stood as our witnesses.

During the days, I cleaned up the garage, which was still full of Kim's moving boxes. I sorted through them one by one, keeping myself occupied just like a good little homemaker.

When I discovered a portable record player, I was excited to play some music. When Kim came home from work, I showed it to him excitedly. But he said, "You can't play it because there are no speakers."

I was depleted and felt stupid. However, the house was taking shape. I was proud that I was making significant progress. I threw myself into making a home for our future family and pushed aside my conflicted feelings about Kim and our relationship.

On weekends we went to the movies—seeing all the big films of the day. I especially remember seeing *The Graduate* and *Guess Who's Coming to Dinner*. Such simple pleasures made me happy. He also introduced me to his colleagues, especially those from Boston, and we were invited to dinners and watched the Red Sox World Series game together at night. I was hooked and have been a Red Sox fan ever since.

Jerrie Witalis, who I got to know more after the wedding, was a great support to me in Indiana and an excellent cook. She taught me how to make spaghetti from scratch, my first American cooking lesson. I also met several neighbors, began to get to know them, and settled into the routine of daily life.

On July 2, 1968, Kevin was born in Indianapolis, again by a cesarean; a healthy boy, almost eight pounds and twenty-one inches long. He brought joy and happiness to our lives. The friends from Boston had given me a baby shower, including a beautiful white crib, and we were fully ready for the baby's arrival. While I was in the hospital, Kim made *miyukguk*—the seaweed soup traditionally offered to a new mother in Korea—and brought it to the hospital in a thermos. I was overwhelmed by his tenderness and thoughtfulness. Kevin was christened at Our Lady of Mount Carmel Catholic Church. Jerrie and Paul Witalis became his godparents, and we became proud parents. God gave me a second chance.

Changes in our lives happened. Now, we were a real family, and I devoted my entire time to Kevin, breastfeeding, bathing, and checking on him every hour to ensure nothing happened to him. He was growing fast into a handsome boy.

My Driving Lesson

In my early years in America, I dreamt about traveling cross-country in a little Volkswagen Beetle with a guitar in the back seat. It didn't seem to concern me that I didn't have a car, didn't know how to drive, and certainly didn't know how to play guitar.

Living on the outskirts of Indianapolis, I couldn't go anywhere without a car. We had only one car—a Volvo 122. It was only a few years old, but the red paint had already faded into a dull pink. It was his car, not ours. Many families had only one car then, so this wasn't unusual.

I badly wanted to drive, but Kim never volunteered to teach me. Instead, he just watched TV on the weekends. So, one weekend, I carefully approached, picking the right moment, and asked Kim to teach me how to drive.

"I will give you the key. Why don't you go out and drive back and forth? Just do it several times, but stay in the driveway. Don't go into the street." He handed me the key while he was watching television. I was disappointed he didn't come out, but I felt relieved that he at least gave me the key.

We lived in a yellow brick ranch house with a two-car garage and a long gravel driveway. The Volvo had a manual transmission. So, I struggled to put the gear in first, drove carefully about fifty yards to the end of the driveway, put the gear in reverse, and backed up. I was so excited that I succeeded on my first try! I drove back and forth in first gear several times, staying in the driveway. Then, backing up, I veered off the driveway and hit something sticking out on the lawn. My heart was pounding fast. Not good. I stopped the car and got out. It was the heating oil pipe for the house. I didn't hit the house, which was good, but that was the end of my self-driving lesson.

I longed for attention and affection, but Kim would rather watch the TV and give the parameters of what I could do. He was almost always indifferent and gave me no attention.

I gave up hope that my husband would teach me, so I called a driving school. The lady instructor was patient and made driving easy with her automatic transmission car. She sat beside me, assuring me she could hit the brakes—an extended one for the instructor—anytime it was needed. We went out to the highway as well as local roads. I felt like I was flying. After several lessons, I got my driver's license on the first attempt! But we still had only one car, the same old Volvo. By then, the car key had broken off inside the ignition. Whenever it stalled at the stop signs, I had to take a screwdriver from the side pocket to restart the car. I was a nervous wreck by the time I made it home. Besides, I could only have the car on weekends or evenings.

Finally, I got my first car, not a Volkswagen Beetle but a beige Volkswagen Squareback—a station wagon—the first year it was introduced in the U.S. It was automatic! Now, there was no way of stopping me. How exhilarating! I got my freedom!

I have been a safe driver for over fifty years, yet I still haven't made that cross-country trip or learned to play the guitar.

EARLY YEARS

Moving, March 1970

In early 1970, PR Mallory's semiconductor division closed its doors after barely three years of operation, and everyone at the company scrambled to find a new job. Luckily, Kim found a new job quickly at RCA's semiconductor division in Somerville, New Jersey, and we had to search for a new home.

Karen was born on December 5, 1969, in Indianapolis. Now, we were a family of four. It was still bitterly cold in early March, and I flew to New Jersey to look for a new house with two kids, Kevin (twenty months old) and Karen (three months old), all bundled up.

RCA had sent a relocation package, which I studied thoroughly and identified several towns to look at. The brochure gave general information about cities, zoning, school systems, population, and education level. I wanted an excellent school system, a population with a high education level, and more land in zoning. However, after talking to real estate agents, I realized a few potential towns were unaffordable for us, and so that quickly eliminated them from our search.

Finally, I found a brand-new house in a new subdivision in Clinton, the western part of New Jersey, and bought it even though it was farther away from Kim's work.

It was a small, quiet town with a waterfall, an old mill, and two buildings by the water, which housed the town's art center and the museum. The main street had several stores: a drug store, a jewelry store, a paint store, a gift shop, a recently opened upscale ladies boutique, and an incredibly contemporary garden furniture and accessory shop. And the elementary school was within walking distance.

The developer built three types of wood-shingled houses—ranch, split-level, and two-story colonial—on an old cow pasture, so there weren't many trees, but the soil was fertile. We bought and moved into a white two-story colonial with four bedrooms on half an acre.

The neighborhood was hilly, and the street name was Quarry Ridge; once there was a quarry behind Spruce Run Road and Hillside Drive, where our house was. However, the backyard was big and leveled, perfect for young children to play, even though the front of the house had a steep driveway sloping down from the street. It was a lovely little town to raise the children in, and most of the neighbors were also young families with kids. It was friendly, too, because everyone was new to the community.

What a stark difference! In Indiana, most houses were brick ranches and looked alike. Our neighbors in Indiana were a little older, and few children were around. The land was as flat as it could be for miles and miles, like in most of the Midwest.

I was a young mother of twenty-eight, staying home to raise the babies, and was happy to make a clean new beginning in a new state back in the East. My enthusiasm for creating a new life lessened the stress of moving.

We lived there for eight years before moving to another township, Tewksbury, but Kevin still remembers his childhood in that house and neighborhood in Clinton. Years later, Kevin told me how he went back and drove by the neighborhood and looked at our old home. It still looked the same, but most neighbors had moved away.

Karen

After all these years, the pain never goes away. I still can't write about it without breaking down. I count how old she would've been on her birthdays if she was still alive. I lost my firstborn baby, and again, I lost another baby. Tragedy struck again. I would instead have switched my life with hers if I could. How could this happen?

I have had recurring dreams that she was dead. I was grieving, holding her lifeless body tight, and then she weakly opened her eyes. She was still alive. I was so happy. I tried to make her strong and not die again. When I woke up, I wished it were real.

It was April 13, 1971, Good Friday. We had an appointment at HR Block to do our tax returns. We got the babysitter, a reliable older woman who had babysat for us. When I brought Karen down to the babysitter, she seemed to have a fever, and I hesitated to leave her. However, since the tax filing deadline was near and I was more familiar with taxes since I did most of the preparation, I decided to go ahead with Kim. It was also a rare occasion for us to go out together, just the two of us, even for an event like this.

It took much longer than we expected. When we returned home late in the afternoon, a neighbor ran to us, telling us to go to the hospital. Karen was sick, and the babysitter had taken Karen in the ambulance. We rushed to the hospital, and when we arrived at the emergency room, they told us that the baby was dead on arrival. I broke down and couldn't remember the rest of what happened. I only remember that they gave me her clothes: a yellow, long-sleeved shirt, all cut up, and a matching yellow corduroy jumper. The clothes looked pathetic somehow, and the baby was dead, but I blamed myself for not dressing her better—how strange the mind can be to even think something like this at that moment. I held on to her clothes and cried and cried. She was sixteen months old.

Later, the doctor told us that they performed the autopsy because of the unusual circumstances of her arrival at the hospital and found that she had died of acute pneumonia.

If I had been more vigilant and stayed home, would I have been able to save her? What was she feeling dying in a stranger's arms? What kind of mother was I? I would rather die with her. But the only strength to live was that I was pregnant and had Kevin to care for.

The old priest who baptized her came by the house the next day. I broke down again. He tried to comfort me with his arms around me, saying *it was God's will.* A few days later, he gave a small funeral service at the funeral home, and I saw Karen's face for the first time since I left her that Friday morning, the same quiet, peaceful look as if she was sleeping. I gave her the rosary I had brought from Korea and could not let her go.

A month after she died, my sweet little girl, I took her picture down from the upstairs hallway. I took all the rest of the photos on the wall down. My hair was falling out, and each morning after showering, I had to scoop the fallen hairs from the floor.

What went wrong? After her birth by cesarean section, it took more than twelve hours for me to wake up from the anesthesia. Did the doctor give me too much anesthesia and harm the unborn baby? Her bedroom windows were facing north and drafty, so I bought heavy vinyl drapes to keep the room warm during the night, but the drapes had chemical smells for a while. I wonder if it might have affected her lungs. Or I traveled with her too early when she was only three months old? I squeezed my brain to figure out what had gone wrong.

She was sick often, but her pediatrician couldn't find anything wrong. She wasn't a year old when her doctor had suggested seeing the cystic fibrosis specialist in Morristown, New Jersey, because her chest cavity seemed bigger than usual. Kim and I were very concerned about the news and the potential outcome. Before our visit, I researched cystic fibrosis in the library, which seemed to be a genetic condition. We made an appointment with the specialist. Kim took a day off from work, and we went to see him. The doctor, in his fifties, seemed friendly and explained the test, which took several hours, to us. We were all exhausted by the time the tests were completed. Finally, he ruled out cystic fibrosis, and we were very relieved. However, he could not come up with any other diagnosis either, and we figured she might have a weaker immune system to the cold. Karen was an otherwise normal but quiet, sweet, gentle baby. She was born full-term and not underweight.

She knew when Kim would come home from work and would tiptoe to the family room picture window, looking out and waiting for her dad daily. She was daddy's little girl.

I stood on the front lawn with Kevin a couple of months after she died. A man carrying a sleeping baby on his shoulder walked by. The baby looked just like Karen, and it took my breath away. And Kevin thought the same, running after him, calling Karen. I had to run inside the house to control myself. What kind of a trick was it?

The week before Karen died, on April 4th, I had received the news that my father had died of a massive stroke. But I couldn't go because I was three months pregnant with two babies at home. How could two deaths happen at the same time? I was still grieving my father's untimely death. Here again, I couldn't breathe. *Had I gone to my father's funeral, would she have lived or still died without me? Did my father take her with him to suffer no more?* There were no answers for me.

She was buried at Fairmont Cemetery in Tewksbury, New Jersey.

COMING HOME

I sing along whenever I hear John Denver's "Take Me Home, Country Roads." It reminded me of my "home far away" in Korea. However, when I listen to the song now, I don't get that melancholy feeling of homesickness it once brought on. I still think of Korea, although now, it's a Korea that exists only in my memory.

One of the happiest days of my life was when I got into Seoul National University (SNU), the most prestigious school in Korea. I was ecstatic and proud. Especially as a female student in a predominantly male-dominated school, I felt like I was the best in the world. My hard work in my studies for all those high school years had paid off.

It was a year after graduation in 1966, that I came to the U.S. for graduate school. I had high hopes of getting my PhD, returning to Korea, and becoming a professor at my alma mater, SNU. But life took a detour, and my dream wasn't realized as I imagined. Instead, I married, had children, and became a stay-at-home mom.

In 1980, fourteen years after I left Korea, Kim was invited to take a senior position in the Korean government's semiconductor research lab—a prestigious group within the Korean Institute of Science and Technology. He was from a prominent Korean family, his father having been a well-known doctor, and he had always longed to return.

He used to lament, "If we lived in Korea, we would be SOMEBODY, but here we are nobody." He was upset about being discriminated against in America, and I hated his constant complaints. I refuted his comments: "If we are outstanding and do much better than others, they will respect us." I indoctrinated my children the same way: "As an Asian, you have to study and work much harder to compete with others in this society."

Presented with a once-in-a-lifetime opportunity like this, we were both very excited, and he accepted the position. His parents in Korea were ecstatic about our return with two grandchildren, Kevin Yungsun and Katherine Yungmee—especially Kevin, the only grandson who would carry the family name.

A couple of years earlier, we had built our dream house and moved from Clinton: a big brick colonial on three acres of woodland in the mountains of Tewksbury Township, New Jersey, well known for its horse farms. It had a fireplace that Kim always wanted and many trees, especially flowering ones like dogwood and mountain laurel, that I always liked. It was so quiet except for the birds chirping, and we couldn't see the neighbors surrounded by the woodlands. It had everything we wanted, including good schools that were most important to me.

However, we were moving again. This time, though, we were going home to Korea. I felt sad leaving behind the lovely house in New Jersey. But at the same time, I was looking forward to returning to Korea. I longed for a close, extended family; this was our opportunity to be immersed in one. In case things didn't work out, we rented the house instead of selling it.

The excitement was building up. My husband's childless older brother, who worked for the Foreign Ministry, enticed us with a house if we returned. He would build a home in the family compound in the most affluent part of Seoul.

We packed a couple of containers full of new furniture, bathroom fixtures, and other building materials unavailable in Korea then, as suggested by his brother, for our new house.

We left in early August 1980 after the children had finished school. On the way, we stopped in Los Angeles and took the kids to Disneyland and Universal Studios. It was our first family vacation like this, and the kids were having a ball. They were thrilled. We also stopped in Honolulu, visited my husband's cousin and her family, and had an excellent island tour, thinking this would be our last time in America.

In Seoul, we moved into a luxury condo in a modern building that the Korean government provided in the bustling Gangnam district, south of the Han River, until the new house was built. That area didn't exist when I left Korea, but now, it is the most sought-after residential and commercial community. What a transformation it was from the war-torn country only thirty years ago! No wonder they call Korea the "Miracle on the Han River!"

Kevin had just finished sixth grade and Katherine finished third grade in America. But in Korea, it was the middle of the semester since the new semester started in March. We debated whether to send our children to an American or a Korean school. Finally, the grandparents firmly said, "The children should enroll in Korean schools to learn how to become real Koreans." The elementary school in the district was supposed to be the best in the city, and we enrolled them in sixth and third grade, repeating the grades they had just finished in America. We thought it would be best for them in the long run.

During one of those early weeks in Korea, Katherine came home from school, sad and disappointed, and said, "Mom, there were many parents at school today for an event, and I was looking for you."

"What kind of event was it?" I was disturbed to have missed it.

"Oh, we played a lot of games. It was fun. I wish you were there."

She thought I should, somehow, have known what was going on at her school.

Later, I discovered it was Student Athletic Day, a fun game event where parents attended and cheered for their children. I felt awful missing this special event for Katherine.

Unfortunately, my children didn't speak Korean, and communication between school and home was challenging. I asked the teachers to give me homework assignments or anything I should know, but it seldom happened.

I hired a tutor to teach them Korean after school, but the tutor was very strict. Even though she was young, in her twenties, her demeanor was rigid, and she dressed conservatively in suits. She instructed my children, "You must address me as 'teacher,' sit straight, and don't fidget during the lessons!"

Occasionally, I looked in to see how it was going, and the children looked bored. On one occasion, when I just happened to peek in, the tutor (or teacher) asked in her frustrated tone, "What is *yuruhgai?*" Kevin looked puzzled and answered hesitantly in English, "Open Dog?" The first time I saw the tutor laugh. It means, in a word, "several." Still, if you split the word into two, *yuruh* means "open" and *gai* means "dog." I experienced similar things in English and understood how intricate learning nuances in a foreign language could be.

Finally, the children had enough and rebelled against her, and she quit. Then, perhaps for the first time, I realized that Kevin and Katherine were Americans. There was a gap, the size of an ocean, in cultural differences between the tutor and my children.

For the children, their favorite part of the day was after school, walking home. Kevin stopped by the bakery and bought pastries and donuts, and Katherine purchased fake Barbie dolls and doll clothes from street vendors at the open market. They were enjoying big city life. What a contrast from life in the mountains of Tewksbury.

In the fall, there were a lot of dragonflies, and my children loved running around on the asphalt parking lot—nearly empty during the day—catching them with nets. After all, there was no need to communicate to play, and they just ran around laughing with neighborhood kids.

This activity was typical for Korean kids, but it was new and fascinating for Katherine and Kevin. The other children were curious about them. Although my children looked Korean, they spoke only English, dressed in blue jeans and T-shirts, and acted like American kids. It's hard to pinpoint exactly how they were different, probably more informal, expressive, and "free range." But they were noticeably out of place. Sometimes, even the guard came out and curiously watched them playing. In contrast, the Korean children were more obedient and respectful and were well aware of their place in the cultural hierarchy. They dressed more formally, too: the boys in pants and button-down shirts, and the girls in dresses.

Kevin learned one thing at school: how to shout *Mansei* (in English, "Hooray"), a group activity where both arms are raised straight up and down repeatedly. He thought that was fun and often exclaimed, "*Mansei*" walking home alone. Korean kids would only do it in a group, not alone.

One of my high school friends, who lived on the first floor of our condo building, said, "I love watching your children playing, especially Kevin shouting *Mansei*." More out of curiosity than in mean spirit.

The children were also proud to see their father driven by a chauffeur commuting in a black Hyundai sedan in the mornings and back home after work, which they were never accustomed to in America.

One day, Kevin brought a friend home, and I was surprised and happy. I offered them cookies and drinks, asked him in Korean about his family, and found out he was an only child with a single mother, which was rare for a Korean family not to have both parents and siblings. They played together briefly, and then the boy wandered around our home. I thought he was bored because Kevin couldn't speak Korean, but I soon found him in my bedroom, taking money out of my purse.

I was heartbroken that the first and only friend Kevin brought home had done this. But to my surprise, Kevin firmly said, "I don't need a friend like him! Get him out of here!" He was only twelve but had already developed a strong moral character. I was proud of my son.

⌐◆⌐

I soon realized that Korea was no longer the "home" of my dreams. The adjustment was difficult not only for the children but for us parents, too. I began to doubt our future in Korea. Living here was different from what we saw during our short vacations.

The promised new house in the upscale neighborhood disappeared in the clouds of family unrest. Kim also realized his work wasn't as prestigious and stimulating as he initially thought it would be. So, we started serious discussions about whether we should return to America before it was too late. Of course, if we went back, his parents would be very disappointed, but the happiness of our family was at stake.

I had missed close-knit family and friends in all my years in America. While I loved seeing my two sisters in Korea and my high school friends, I missed the American independence and openness of an unburdened lifestyle. I also realized how much I had changed in fourteen years. Furthermore, besides two sisters, the rest of the family by that stage had emigrated to America, including my mother.

Kim went to see his parents alone and told them things weren't working out and that we were considering returning to America. They urged Kim to reconsider and believed that we should stay in Korea. He told me later that they were more upset than surprised.

It was more like a threat to us, especially from his brother, who worked in the Korean Foreign Ministry. He served as Korea's ambassador to Ecuador and Belgium and was well-connected to the Korean government. We were afraid that he might use his muscle of government connections on his parents' behalf to prevent us from leaving.

I completely understood then what my husband used to say, "My brother was a bully when he was young. And whenever we fought over my toys, my parents always sided with my brother, saying, 'Just give it to him.'"

Now, I felt sorry for my husband, how his brother bullied him, never shared anything, and how he was unfairly treated by his parents when they were growing up. And the dynamic still hadn't changed.

Shortly afterward, I was summoned by one of my husband's uncles, who was once the Home Minister and well-respected by the family. I explained to him, "Things are not working out as we had hoped. The promised house disappeared. I don't see any inheritance coming our way, either. Everything seems already in my husband's brother's name, and he seems unwilling to share anything. Furthermore, the children are struggling in a Korean school."

I was pouring out my grievances and frustrations to him. He listened quietly and seemed to understand my logic of wanting to return.

He finally spoke, "Now I understand. I will talk to my sister [my mother-in-law]."

And he paused, "You are a smart woman."

I was surprised to hear his comment because elders seldom praise younger people in Korea, especially females. However, he didn't try to stop us from leaving.

My mother-in-law called me after I met with her brother, and I went to see her alone. It was a one-on-one meeting, just for her and me. She said, "Emyung [the older brother] has no children. So, when he dies, all his inheritance will go to your children. So, don't feel bad. Besides, I have a renewed hope that you can work with me. I can guide you."

She was once a very active woman, unusual in her generation in Korea, accumulating the family fortune in real estate and the stock market until a mysterious illness struck her. She lost her ability to walk and was wheelchair-bound.

She was pleading with me to stay. She was very reserved, and I never knew what she thought of me. I was surprised to hear her confidence in me and her secret plan to become active again, working with me, her daughter-in-law, even though she had two daughters of her own and an older daughter-in-law.

However, we had already decided to return to America and quietly planned the logistics without telling his family anything further. We decided to call his parents later once we were safely back in America. I sold most things through my friends and sisters, and packed the basics to bring back with us.

Finally, we bought the plane tickets, which happened to be on Thanksgiving Day in America. It had been three short, extremely hectic months in Korea struggling to figure out how to make a home, and finally deciding to return to America.

The Gimpo Airport, outside Seoul, was nearly deserted early in the morning, and we looked around the airport like criminals escaping secretly, just in case his brother showed up with the police. That could happen. The kids didn't quite know what was happening, but they were happy that we were returning home, their real home, in New Jersey. With the holiday, the plane was nearly empty except for a rabbi sitting alone in the back seat and a few others— it was just like we were in a private plane.

Finally, I felt calm, with a sense of regret that things didn't work out as we had hoped, but I also had renewed resolve—no more "what-ifs." America is our home, and I will make it in America! It was a most pivotal moment—no turning back. We came back—home!

NEW START

Resettling—1981

It was a bitterly cold day in late November, after Thanksgiving, when we returned from Korea. The trees were bare, and hay bales sat in rows amidst fields like a scene from a Monet painting. I took the children back to Tewksbury Township, New Jersey, where they had attended schools before we left just three months earlier, though it felt much longer.

"You just made it in time," Mrs. Smith, the kind-looking school principal with cropped gray hair, said.

"If you were a couple of weeks later, your children would have missed a grade and been a year behind."

So, Kevin was back in the seventh grade at Old Turnpike Middle School, and Katherine was in the fourth grade at the Sawmill School. They were happy to return to a familiar environment with their old friends. They lost three months of a new semester but were intelligent kids and could catch up.

We couldn't return to our house because we'd rented it with a two-year lease to a British couple—the wife had been transferred to New Jersey for a university position. But we found a big five-bedroom contemporary-style house in the same town for rent, next to the horse farm for which Tewksbury is known. The Town Hall was nearby and closer to the children's schools. The owners were transferred to Australia and stored everything in the basement, including their furniture. Since Kim was looking for a job, our future was uncertain, and we had no idea where we'd ultimately be. The only furniture we bought were beds for each bedroom on the first floor.

I gave Kevin and Katherine their choice of one piece of furniture for their room. Katherine picked a French-style white canopied bedroom set from the Sears catalog, and Kevin chose a maple desk. He was always considerate, practical, and frugal, while Katherine tested her limits.

Kim couldn't or didn't want to return to his old job in New Jersey. Fortunately, he found a new job at Digital Equipment Corporation's (DEC) semiconductor plant in Hudson, Massachusetts. It was the early 1980s, and the computer industry was booming in Massachusetts, and Route 128 was known as "America's Technology Highway."

I was excited about returning to where Kim and I met when I first came to school fifteen years ago. It felt like going back home. He still had many Korean friends and was happy to be going back too.

DEC sent us a relocation package. I read everything carefully—like studying for the college entrance exam! After much consideration, I chose two towns to look at, Harvard and Lincoln, based on my evaluation of their population, education level, income, school ratings, zoning regulations, and the distance to work. After all, economic geography was my major, and industrial site analysis and location studies were my favorite subjects! As it turned out, I went to Harvard first, fell in love with the town, and didn't even bother going to Lincoln.

In the summer of 1981, after the children finished their school year in New Jersey, we finally moved to the picturesque, small New England town of Harvard, Massachusetts, thirty-odd miles west of Boston. Harvard was best known for its apple orchards and was often featured in national magazines as the most beautiful town in New England. The town center was called the "Commons." It was surrounded by a general store combined with a drug store; the town library; several centuries-old houses; and Catholic, Congregational, and Unitarian churches located prominently at the head of the Commons, each with a beautiful white steeple. It even had a town pond called Bare Hill Pond, where the kids swam.

The Bromfield School, K-12 with about nine hundred students, was all on one campus. It was a public school, but it was not regionalized and had an excellent reputation.

The town's highest point housed the Fruitlands Shaker Museum with a sweeping view of Nashoba Valley. The transcendentalist Amos Bronson Alcott, Louisa May Alcott's father, once tried establishing a utopian village on that ground.

We bought a three-year-old, two-story colonial house with two acres on Ann Lee Road in the Shaker Hills section of town, named after Mother Ann Lee, the founder of the Shakers. In the back of the house, sloping down to woodlands, a walking trail led to nearby old Shaker dancing and burial grounds. Dancing was their ritual; hence, the name Shaker. I always remembered, particularly in the fall, how beautiful the trees were with brilliant reds and yellows and the feeling of every step cushioned by fallen leaves underfoot.

After the first day of school, I drove to pick up the kids and waited behind the school buses at the curbside. A policeman approached me. I was nervous, wondering what I was doing wrong.

I thought about last fall when we left Korea; we hadn't done anything wrong but feared encountering the police at the airport just in case they arrested us for leaving.

"You must be Mrs. Kim," he said.

"How do you know me?" I was surprised he knew who I was, especially since we were new. *But maybe it was because we were the only Asian family in town.*

"Welcome to Harvard! I just wanted to welcome you," he said.

I quickly learned how small a town Harvard was. Everyone knew everyone else.

Searching for a Job—from 1981 to 1983

Kevin was in the eighth grade, and Katherine was in fifth. I planned to send Kevin to a boarding school when he began high school, and I needed a job because we couldn't afford it with Kim's salary alone.

I was anxious to start working. I hadn't been in any professional field for a long time by this stage and was willing to get whatever I could.

Even so, I still harbored a desire to have my own business. It was something I'd always dreamed of. Going back to the early 1970s, when the children were little, I started a toy import business from home, importing stuffed toys from Korea and selling them wholesale to department stores.

I also worked for the U.S. Postal Service (USPS). One day, while I was working there, a Postal Inspector arrived. Everyone was on their best behavior. Then the postmaster came out and said, gesturing toward me, "Please go to my office. The Postal Inspector wants to see you." I didn't know what was going on. I was a new employee, and everyone looked at me like I was a spy!

However, when I went in, the inspector smiled and said, "Please sit. I have something to discuss with you." So, I sat down like a student called into the principal's office.

"You did very well on your Postal exam. We haven't seen anyone who did so well. So, I checked your background, and we are interested in you for another position in the Postal Service." Hearing this, I sighed in relief that I wasn't in trouble and was ready for what he had to offer. He explained that a job was available as a Federal Agent in a prominent Korean community in Los Angeles. He also said, "You can retire in twenty-five years with a good pension. However, you need to carry a gun." That scared me a little.

However, I knew immediately that Kim wouldn't let me take that kind of job and would object to us moving—so I explained that it wasn't possible.

While looking for a suitable job, I applied for a substitute teacher position at Bromfield, my children's school. I taught geography at Girls' High School in Korea for a year before coming to America. I also did substitute teaching in social studies at New Jersey high schools while my kids were little.

With my background in teaching, the school called me frequently, especially on bad weather days during the wintertime when many of the staff were away. I was almost working full-time at the school during the winter, so this kept me busy. As a result, I got to know the school well. I had always been self-conscious about the fact we were the only Asian family at the school, and I didn't want my children to be discriminated against. I thought that, by being a teacher at the school, the other teachers might get to know me and, in turn, make sure my children were treated well.

When a position came up at the school unexpectedly, they asked me to take over the American history high school class for the remaining term, and I did. I went to the school library, borrowed several textbooks on American history, and studied every night to prepare for the class. And I realized that teaching was the best way to learn.

Whenever we'd moved houses over the years, the agents would say I'd be great in real estate. I kept that in mind as it was something that I wanted to try someday. Finally, the opportunity came. I found a real estate course advertised in the local paper, took it, passed the exam, and got my sales license. Soon after, I saw an ad in the Boston Globe; Hunneman, a prominent Boston real estate firm, had opened a new office in Groton, Massachusetts, and was looking for salespeople. It was close to home. I interviewed and became the first person to work in that office. I loved interacting with people and especially liked helping new transferees find their new home. It felt different from the other part-time work I'd had. For one, Kim hadn't objected to it—perhaps because he didn't find it threatening—yet there was still the potential to make good money. There was a freedom to this job for me—it felt like it was the first step to an actual career. My children still joke about how I dragged them to open houses every weekend when they were little.

I was good at finding the right home for each of my clients. I remember a new client walking into the office very early on. He'd been transferred to New England and sought a family home. I quickly found the exact type of house he was after—a brand-new colonial just on the market—and sold it to him. It was the second house that I'd shown him.

The next day, the manager called me into his office. I thought he was going to praise me for the quick sale. Instead, he said, "A few people in the office were complaining that you don't come in the office full-time like them, and you made a sale so quickly." He was warning me that people were envious. He also added, "Making a sale that quick is not good. Then, you would think 'sale' is easy. But there can be a famine for many months." However, I also saw the investment opportunities since the agents got to see the listings first. A man in the office had mentioned that was how you made money rather than just sales in real estate.

The school semester had ended, and I thought of working full-time in real estate. Remember the three most essential things in real estate? Location, location, and location. I was a geographer studying the subject of "location!"

I also looked for a career in the field of geography. Geography had always been my passion, and I still dreamt of finding a job in this field. One day, I saw an ad from a well-known computer-aided design and mapping technology company in the Boston area looking for a sales and marketing person, and I applied. Soon, I got a call from a person at the company looking for "Mister" Kija Kim. I answered excitedly, "This is she." There was silence on the other end of the line. I wasn't surprised; I often get mistaken for "Mister Kija Kim," even today.

To make a long story short, I didn't even have a chance to get interviewed. It was clear that he had a man in mind for the job. What a significant loss for them! I could have been the best salesperson that the company ever had. In hindsight, Kim would have objected even if I got the job. Whenever I had an opportunity to pursue a position that might lead to a career, Kim vehemently opposed it and made me feel guilty for even trying. A cartography job came up in New Jersey that I interviewed for. Another time, I went out for a job interview during the day. It was for a new position that was computer mapping-related. I came home very excited. Kim was outraged that I went without telling him. Of course, I hadn't told him as I knew he wouldn't even let me apply. It happened several times more before I gave up. It was a way he could exert control over me, and I also think he was afraid of me becoming more successful than him and leaving him.

At the same time I was looking for a job, the Bromfield School math teacher, who also taught a computer science class at nearby Fitchburg State College, told me he was starting a night class for computer programming at Bromfield. I wasn't afraid of learning new things. I took courses in computer programming in BASIC and, later, computer-aided design (CAD). I didn't know it at the time, but this night course was going to prove invaluable to me in the years to come.

Looking back at everything I have done, from waitressing to importing stuffed toys to delivering mail to teaching American history, nothing has been wasted, and every step has taken me to where I am today. That's how I became so immersed in American life, taking any chance I could and adapting to every job I could get! I still tell my children and grandchildren to seize every opportunity; life is lived one step at a time.

～

In between job hunting, I created a project. I was restless. The master bedroom wallpaper was dark green, making the room depressing. I decided to take the wallpaper off and paint the room. I had never done it before but figured it wouldn't be rocket science. I wet the wallpaper, panel by panel, let them soak, and started peeling them off.

What a surprise! There was another wallpaper underneath, big red flowers on a beige background, a somewhat Asian motif. I couldn't believe how they covered such beautiful wallpaper with an ugly green one. I was so energized by the discovery that I couldn't stop working all day until the entire room was done. This project occupied me for a couple of weeks and lifted my spirit. The master bedroom was entirely transformed and bright!

The revelation of the beautiful wallpaper in the master bedroom made me think, at least at some subconscious level, that beauty could be found within this house. I just had to see it—if I could transform this house, room by room, perhaps I could also transform it into a happy home for my family.

First Christmas

After returning to America, Kim often went to Korea alone during the holidays to be with his parents, leaving me and the children alone. His father's birthday happened to be Christmas Day, which was a good excuse for leaving at this time of year. *Did he feel guilty returning to America to live and disappointing his parents?* He tried hard to please them, even at the cost of his own family. Looking back, I think he always harbored a desperate desire to be loved by them. The tragedy of Kim's life was that, in the end, he lost everything. He never felt loved by his parents, and with his efforts focused on seeking their love, he never saw what was right in front of him; he never learned to become a loving father and husband.

Christmas in 1981, the first year we moved to Massachusetts, Kim left for Korea. I felt terrible for the kids having to spend the biggest holiday without their father, but I tried to make the best of it.

"Hey, let's go to the back of the house and find a Christmas tree." I encouraged them to come along. The house was on two acres of woodland sloping down to the trail behind.

"No, I don't want to. You go ahead if you want." Kevin was upset. Katherine didn't even respond. Christmas was already spoiled, and they weren't in any mood to participate in my effort. I hesitated about what to do but decided to go ahead by myself.

No snow was on the ground, and it was a crisp, clear winter day. I dressed warmly in a double-lined short coat and jeans, put on my boots, found a hacksaw in the garage, and set off down the hill. The earth was cushiony but slippery with wet fallen leaves. I looked for decent-looking pine or spruce to cut, but most were too small, too big, or out of shape. I finally found one that looked decent. It was about five feet tall with a small trunk, but it took a long time for me to cut it down with a hacksaw. Finally, I dragged it uphill to the living room.

"How does it look? You can help me decorate it." I still wanted the children to engage. "It's Christmas!"

"It looks pathetic!" Kevin said as he stormed out of the living room. Katherine went to her room and closed the door. I felt like crying, but I held my breath and stood there. Inside, the tree looked thinner and somehow more distorted than it looked outside. But I didn't want to give up. If I did, it would be a disaster. So, I went to the attic, brought down the Christmas ornaments, sat down, and decorated the tree alone.

∽∼

Kevin and I went to Logan Airport to meet Kim, returning from Korea after the Christmas holiday, and waited in the car for his arrival at the gate. Kevin moved to the back seat so his father could sit in the front. The airport was crowded with post-holiday travelers.

"Here's Dad!" Kevin saw him first and was excited. Once his dad spotted our Volvo station wagon, he approached, opened the passenger door, and jumped in. Before saying a word, he hit me in the face. Kevin was scared, frozen in the backseat. I could smell the liquor on his breath. I was wearing glasses, and they fell and broke, cutting my cheek. I still have a small scar on my left cheek, never erasable, as a reminder of that time.

"Where were you all day?" he yelled. "I have been trying to call you the entire time, and the line was busy." He tried to call during the transfer plane in Alaska, but the line was busy because Katherine was on the phone all day with her friends—that's how she blocked out the lonely feeling of the quiet, empty house.

I couldn't drive without my glasses, and he drove while we kept silent during the entire trip home.

TURNING POINT

Around this same time, the early 1980s, Kim fell into depression and other mental health issues exacerbated by his heavy drinking. To cope, I focused on the children and blocked out everything else. However, every day when Kim got home from work, the first thing he did was take out the bottle of whiskey and start pouring. Dinner time was getting quieter and quieter, and I was afraid of triggering his anger. He also developed a phobia of driving on highways, and it took twice as long to get to his work on small secondary roads. He was also paranoid. He sometimes came home early unexpectedly, and if I was not home, he got agitated and became violent.

The children and I treaded quietly so as not to provoke his anger that might detonate at anytime. No confrontation became our norm, falsely thinking we could maintain the peace that way.

He desperately needed help. I suggested that he should seek professional help. But, of course, he balked at the idea.

"Do you think I am crazy? What are you trying to do? Are you trying to put me in the mental hospital?" He was angry, screaming.

I was desperate and saw our family doctor in Acton. And I explained Kim's problems and symptoms and asked for help.

It was my first big step and a significant turning point for me.

After listening quietly, he said, "I can't help him unless he takes the first step. Nobody can help him unless he realizes he needs help. But I can help you because you came asking for help." Then, he told me to go and see a psychologist. Although at some level I resisted, in my heart I knew I had no other option but to follow his advice. I made myself an appointment with the psychologist.

Of course, Kim soon learned about this and was very upset and dead against it. But, by this point, I was determined to go. Often, he came home early from work on my appointment day and blocked the driveway to prevent me from going. My memories are hazy, but I missed several meetings that way.

I think the psychologist's name was Dr. Schnyder; I'm not sure now, but he was younger than I expected, maybe in his late thirties. His office was a little cluttered and dark—it wasn't sunny. It was more like going to a doctor's office than the shrinks you see in the movies! But what he told me in those sessions is still vivid.

"I failed my parents. I promised them I would get my PhD, return to Korea, and become a professor. I'm still getting nightmares about how I failed and I feel ashamed," I told him in one of the sessions. He was an excellent listener, attentive, and kind. He only made comments occasionally, but they were always very impactful to me.

"You failed YOUR expectations, not theirs," he said sternly, looking straight into my eyes. I realized at that moment that he was right. The heavy guilt and shame that I carried for so long was lifted.

"Why don't you leave him?" he asked in another session.

I paused and said, "What will I do with the children? I can't leave him. I don't have any financial means to support them."

Then he said, "There are a lot of women out there who are less educated and less able than you, who work and raise the kids by themselves. So why can't you?"

It was a pivotal moment for me. I started to see myself in a different light. It was the beginning of a rediscovery of my true self. I saw perhaps clearly for the first time how the years with Kim had eroded my self-confidence. *Where was the girl who stepped onto the plane for America to go and study? Where had she gone?* At that moment, I realized I could take the steps to financial independence. I felt guilty that I hadn't protected the children from their father's abuse for so long. I would get a job. It was the beginning of my serious job search.

MY CAREER IN COMPUTER MAPPING

In the fall of 1982, I finally got a job as a cartographer at a civil engineering and surveying firm, Charles Perkins Company, in Clinton, Massachusetts.

However, I didn't want to give up my new career in real estate. So, I asked to work from Monday through Thursday at Perkins and in the real estate office on weekends, Friday, Saturday, and Sunday. The weekend was the busiest time in the real estate business anyway, and both companies agreed to my schedule.

The job at Perkins was tedious with manually drawing maps. I thought there had to be a better way to automate the mapmaking process, or Automated Mapping, as it would soon be known. I asked the surveyors and engineers to explain the process from data collection to mapping in detail.

The early 1980s was an exciting time with the emergence of Microsoft, personal computers, and computer-aided design (CAD) software. The technological revolution was happening.

Even with my limited training in programming and CAD, I could see the possibilities to automate mapmaking; putting together hardware and software. The large format digitizing table and printer and new CAD software, such as AutoCAD, were available. It was a matter of how they could be interfaced. I attended a few conferences on automation, had an idea of how it could be done, and brought my vision to the owners. I tried to persuade them to give me a chance, but they repeatedly said, "No." They felt it would be too much "up-front capital investment." But I didn't give up and kept pushing my ideas.

One day, to my surprise, one of the men who had been in my computer class at Bromfield walked into the office. I immediately recognized Mr. Goldstein—he always wore blue jeans and a leather jacket. I knew he was a prominent developer and lived in the same town as me, but I hadn't known he was an important company client.

"Hey, Kija! I didn't know you worked here." And, turning his head toward me, he said to Mr. McDougal, a partner of the company, "We took a computer class together." At that moment, something changed in Mr. McDougal—he looked at me differently. Perhaps Mr. Goldstein had provided the validation for my capabilities? That conversation sparked something. A few weeks later, one of the partners approached me and said they were interested in my idea.

The company invested in the system, hardware, and software and built a separate room for me with a glass enclosure to house the system at the corner of the large open main floor, where engineers, surveyors, and drafters worked. And I was a one-person CAD Division head. Other employees were awed by my progress; some were envious and jabbed that the room looked like a bank vault. The drafters worried about losing their jobs through automation, but some wanted to work for me to learn how to get into the game early. It was an exciting time for me and the company.

The company's partners were proud of the new automated mapping system and brought clients and friends to see it. They thought it was magical. Some suggested we should offer other companies a "computerized mapping service." Then, I saw it could potentially be a standalone business. And I started discussing with the owners to set up a separate company as a partnership to offer this service to many other companies to "leverage the investment" they had made.

I would become an equity partner and the president, and run the operation of this new company, but I needed their investment and network to bring business.

Again, the partners said, "No." This time, they saw the system as their "competitive advantage" and didn't want to offer the services to other companies. But I was patient.

A few months later, they agreed to the idea. Again, something happened. They thought separating this new company could be a hedge/shield from potential lawsuits against the mother company. I finally felt that this could be a real opportunity to become a partner in the firm and started formulating the idea of building a business.

Through a friend, I talked to a Harvard Business School professor, Jeff Timmons, who lived in the same town, about starting a new business. Professor Timmons introduced me to one of Boston's top lawyers and accountants. He also recommended reading an excellent book on entrepreneurship, his own *New Venture Creation*. I studied it from cover to cover. New venture formation was moving fast.

In the early 1980s, there were primarily white men and a few women in engineering. I was the only Asian and minority in the company. However, I became an expert in automated mapping, got along well with the managers, helped their workload with automation, and changed the workflow process. In addition, I brought innovative ideas to help the organization. It was a win-win.

Then, one day, the two partners, one civil engineer and another surveyor who had bought the company from the founder several years earlier, called me into the office.

"We have been discussing the new venture concept with our company accountant and lawyer." They didn't know how to approach the subject, but I felt it wasn't good. The bottom line was that their accountant and lawyer advised the owners that they didn't have to give up any company's equity and should hire me to run the company. All my planning and hard work to be a partner for a new venture seemed to evaporate at that moment. The deal fell through, and I was very disappointed. Later, I learned that's what happens when the lawyers and the accountants get involved.

I declined their offer. Since I had come this far, I couldn't think of going back and working for them. Instead, I would try to do this by myself, turn this negative situation into a positive one, and capitalize on this opportunity.

Opportunity comes to prepared minds. My mantra!

In 1984, I left Perkins and started my own consulting business, New England Mapping Company, to offer automated mapping services for civil engineering firms.

Time passed, and one day, Mr. Larry Allen, CEO of a prominent Boston-based engineering, surveying, and architectural company, ADMN, visited me and asked if I could set up an automated mapping system for his company. We discussed his needs and what he was trying to accomplish. I signed a one-month contract to set up the system and train the staff.

I still lived in Harvard, Massachusetts, about thirty-four miles west of Boston, and had to commute the distance every day. I turned on the classical music station on the radio to bring some joy to the long drive. However, the highlight of commuting was watching the scullers rowing on the Charles River on Storrow Drive. So peaceful!

ADMN's office was at Copley Square in Back Bay, Boston, across from the John Hancock building, and occupied the top two floors of a six-story building. It had over eighty employees: engineers, surveyors, architects, and administrative staff. They set aside ample space for me to set up the system on the corner of the main floor and provided me with a parking spot, which was valuable in the city.

I later learned that ADMN was the last initials of the four partners. The work went well, duplicating my system, testing, and generating maps. Like at Perkins, people were curious and fascinated, and Mr. Allen came to see me often and was satisfied with the operation, the result of his pioneering spirit.

⌒〜

Toward the end of my contract, Mr. Allen and Mr. Major, the executive vice president, invited me to lunch at the University Club in Boston, around the corner from our office.

The University Club was Boston's premier social and athletic club. The dining room was warm and inviting with mahogany-paneled walls, leather chairs, and alabaster pendant chandeliers hanging low. Well-dressed service staff paid close attention to the guests. I noticed most diners were business people, and I was the only woman in the room.

I thought it was to celebrate the successful end of my contract. However, they asked if I could join their management team running the Automated Mapping Division.

"We know you provided good training, but no one could operate the system well enough without you," they said.

I realized I had no "old-boy network" to succeed by then. I didn't have high school friends, college roommates, or family members to help. Being an Asian woman and an immigrant, the lack of a network was a significant barrier to building my business, and marketing was difficult without connections.

I saw this opportunity to revive my dream of eventually starting a new company, which I had initially offered at the previous company. So, during lunch, I asked, "When the time comes, would you consider separating the division into an independent company?" First, I wanted to see if they would like the idea.

"Of course, we will consider it if the timing is right." They were interested. I knew the concept was premature, but I planted an idea to think about.

Now, we had to negotiate the salary. "Do you have in mind what salary you would consider?" They approached me carefully. I thought for a minute and said, "How about $40,000?" I considered it a good starting salary.

"Done deal!" they both said immediately without any hesitation. But then, I realized I had undersold myself. I was kicking myself, but it was too late. Nonetheless, I was happy with the outcome. But I learned the lesson to check what they were willing to pay first and then negotiate.

I agreed to join the firm, thinking I would be better prepared to have a partner next time. Now, I became a member of the management team of a big company and regularly attended management meetings where I learned about running the business and avoiding pitfalls.

DISINTEGRATION
OF THE MARRIAGE

It was the summer of 1987, and the children were off
school. Kim's company had an outing planned, a weekend cruise to Nova Scotia. The children and I were excited
and looked forward to this mini-vacation—we seldom had
family time together to enjoy ourselves. We packed a couple
of overnight bags and dressed for a cruise. The kids were in
jeans and collared shirts, and I wore long khaki pants and
a white shirt, carrying extra sweaters and hats for everyone. We drove from Harvard, Massachusetts, to Portland,
Maine. Many families were waiting for the boat when we
arrived at the port, but I didn't see anyone we knew.

After we got on board, we found our cabin and settled
in. It was a perfect summer afternoon with a clear blue sky,
families with kids milling around the deck, and we were all
enjoying the views from the water in anticipation of a fun
trip ahead.

However, once the ship was on open seas, the gambling started. Kim went directly to the gambling table and
started drinking.

Kevin and I begged him not to drink and to return to
the cabin, but he was already drunk and yelled at us to
disappear. We returned to our cabin helplessly, leaving him
behind. However, Katherine was worried about her father
and went back out to look after him. I laid down on the

cabin bed, fuming. A while later, Katherine ran in crying, telling us he'd fallen to the floor. Kevin and I went to see what was happening, with Katherine following behind. I could not believe the scene—his body slumped on the floor like a dead person. Kevin and I stood there in shock, trying to figure out what to do. Finally, each pulling his arms, Kevin and I dragged him back to the cabin while others watched us in sympathy.

The kids and I were publicly humiliated by his drunkenness, and we were all too upset to sleep. We arrived in Nova Scotia at dawn the following day, and the air was chilly. However, we had no desire for sightseeing. The entire trip was already ruined. Furthermore, I couldn't face the people who looked at us peculiarly or with sympathy. The trip we were so looking forward to ended in a disaster. It broke my heart. At this point, I had enough; no more turning back.

~~

The frayed rope that held our marriage together was finally breaking. I packed my bags and left with the kids. It was not the first time I had done so. I had been trying to leave the marriage many times before but never had the financial resources to carry it through. I remember running away years earlier when we lived in New Jersey. Halfway to my brother's house in Penn Yan, upstate New York, I was at a gas station filling the car, and the children kept asking me *where are we going?* I had no answers. Thinking about the kids and what was best for them, it felt easier to turn around and return home. And I did. So, through all those years, I kept coming back.

I still worried about the children, even though they were in high school and college and no longer little. I didn't want to unsettle them. So many thoughts raced around and around my head: *Would any Korean family allow their child to marry the child of a divorced mother? How can I tell my mother that I am going to divorce? Would my brother or sister take me in with the kids if I needed their help? What could be worse than living like this? I am suffocating.*

I kept everything secret, though, within the bounds of my household and inside the family. I didn't want anybody to know.

It was a family matter.

However, one morning, I was having a cup of coffee with my next-door neighbor, and she brought up my husband and said, looking at me straight, "You only live once, you know." I didn't respond, pretending I didn't hear her, but her words kept ringing.

At least I had a job managing the automated mapping division for an engineering company in Boston. However, the company was going under with the real estate market collapse in Boston in 1987, and I knew it was just a matter of time. I wanted to start my own business, but Kim objected to it as he always did.

"Dad, give Mom a chance. She might succeed!" my son said, pleading when he heard our argument in the kitchen. He was home from college during spring break.

Perhaps that's what my husband was afraid of, my success, and then I might leave him.

I went through many sleepless nights thinking and rethinking what choices I had. *What about the children?*

Wouldn't they be better off without an abusive and alcoholic father? Didn't I send Kevin off to boarding school for him to get away from his father? And for myself? I want to live my life.

~~

When I decided to divorce, I went to see my mother. However, I was afraid of her reaction, took a deep breath and said hesitantly, "I've decided to get a divorce, Mom."

"What took you so long?" was her first response, as if she had been expecting it for a long time. I felt so relieved and thankful for her consent without any questions.

Years later, as the board chairwoman for the Asian Task Force Against Domestic Violence, I visited their shelter/safe house in Boston. A skinny Asian woman came in holding a little girl's hand, with a little boy following. She was pulling a small suitcase. I was frozen, *that's me*, I said to myself. How often had I run away to dirty motels with the kids when I didn't have a place to turn to?

After my divorce, I had two calls from Korean friends in Boston. One, a doctor herself and also married to a doctor, called me and said, "You gave me the courage, and I filed for divorce." I never knew they had a difficult marriage. And I was shocked, as divorce is so shameful in Korean culture. Then another woman—her scientist husband was Kim's high school classmate in Korea—saw me on television testifying about education reform in Massachusetts and said how proud she was of me.

Until then, I still carried the shame of divorce. But I now realized people were proud of me, and the guilt was lifted.

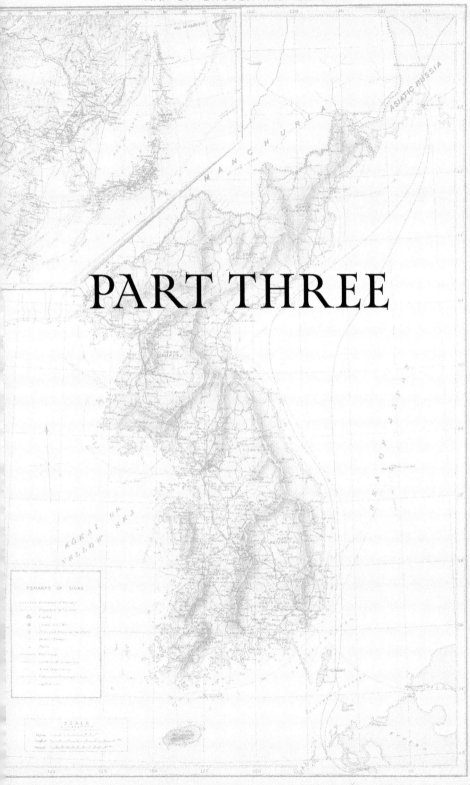

PART THREE

ENDINGS AND BEGINNINGS

When I got the job at ADMN, we were briefly happy. Kim was probably surprised about what the money from my wage could bring. So, he bought a brand-new Mercedes Benz station wagon—the first time we had such a luxury car. The kids were happy, too. But then he had a mental breakdown, collapsing at the dinner table, talking about death constantly, and having a phobia about driving. Our happiness was short-lived.

When I started HDM, my own company, I was at a breaking point in my marriage. It was shortly after the company boat trip that I asked for a divorce. Katherine was in her senior year at high school, a tough year with all the upheaval at home. The children are survivors, too.

The hardest part for me was how Kim manipulated the children against me, telling them I was the bad one breaking up the family and he was the victim of my actions. But I endured it because I didn't want them to suffer more.

There weren't many assets to divide except the real estate. A few years earlier, I helped Kim's friend from Korea find a condo for his son, who was a college student in Boston. Around the same time, Kim and I bought a condo in a new building on the Cambridge/Watertown line overlooking the Charles River. It was a suitable investment property.

When we were divorcing, I told him I would take the condo since it was closer to my work in Cambridge, and he could take the house in Harvard, which was closer to his work. The two properties were of about equal value with similar mortgages. He refused. So, I kept the Harvard house; he, the Cambridge condo. He kept all his pensions and retirement funds. He even cleared our joint bank account even though it wasn't significant. I just wanted to get over it, and I agreed to that to devote time to my new business.

I had a long drive home from Cambridge and arrived late most nights. We were officially separated, waiting for the divorce to be finalized. However, Kim was constantly stalking me. It scared me to death. Even before then, he came around and took the air out of my car's tires at night while I was sleeping. As Kim would be lurking and waiting for me, I filed a restraining order, and he countered by filing a restraining order against me, too. I had always been a victim in my marriage, and now I started fighting back. Kim made the divorce difficult.

In 1991, after three long, painful years of divorce proceedings, twenty difficult years of marriage, and the divorce was finalized.

He had a lovely family, but because of his many demons, he was blind to them and lost everything. That was the biggest tragedy and it was particularly heartbreaking for the children to live through it.

Even though this time was difficult, it was also a time of significant personal growth for me. I had to find such enormous inner strength to keep going. It was also essential for me to have my own financial means. Before, when I was dependent on Kim, I was very frugal, making my clothes and shopping at discount stores. Finally, I could shop—buying white linen pants and suits at Ann Taylor's.

Some people commented on how fashionable I looked. I felt good about myself.

After the divorce, I felt liberated, no longer living in constant fear. I wanted to live my authentic life and embrace my independence! How can you transform if you can't seek an authentic life?

With the 1987 stock market crash, the real estate industry in Boston also started to collapse. Many real estate developers went bankrupt. The company I worked for was in big trouble because they co-invested money and their employee's time into many real estate development projects in exchange for equity. That equity came with significant risk. We had many management meetings to rescue the company, drowning with uncollectible receivables.

I went to see Larry Allen, the CEO, to revive my earlier idea of setting up a new company. Despite the market downturn, I thought the timing was right. Mr. Allen pushed aside the papers he was working on and said with a polite smile, "Please take a seat," showing me the chair across from his desk.

I could see he had a lot on his mind. I sat down, surveying his office, the framed professional licenses on the wall, and family photos on the credenza behind his desk.

I took a moment to assess my approach. Carefully, I reminded him about our original discussion—turning my division into a new company.

He listened attentively and said, "I'll think about it and get back to you. Is next week okay?" He seemed serious, and I left his office feeling optimistic.

When I joined ADMN in early 1986, two young guys—a geologist and a researcher, Bill and Jim—were in the office next to mine. They weren't in the office much as they worked outside most of the day. Jim was always dressed impeccably in suits and ties and wore a brown cashmere winter coat, while Bill wore jeans and work boots to go to the wetlands. Jim frequently visited the state and local cities and towns, researching the title and zoning for the company's real estate division. He made a significant career change from government to this research work, his first foray into the private sector. He joined the company shortly before me, so he was also new.

There were social events in the company—I had a Halloween party at our house in Harvard and invited some company people. Larry came in a whole Dracula outfit with makeup and everything, along with his wife, not in costume. Others came from far away, including Jim. It was a fun evening. Another time, Jim hosted a party for Bill's farewell—they were good friends—inviting mostly company people, and I came along, too. I got to know the company people well through these parties, especially Jim and Bill. I remember one occasion I brought a holiday rice cake from home. I wanted to share it with everyone—they were all curious about its taste. However, Jim politely declined, saying, "I am not very brave with new kinds of food!"

A month passed, and Larry still didn't get back to me. I became anxious. Jim was curious about my meetings with Larry. At one point, I confided in Jim about my plan for new business negotiations. Over those few months, I noticed that Jim paid a lot of attention to what I was doing at the office—he wanted to learn about the various projects I was working on and kept asking about how the negotiation with Larry was going. I told him later that I didn't think it would work out as it was over a month since I'd talked to Larry, and he'd delegated my business plan to the CFO. I still remember this conversation with Jim so clearly.

"I'm thinking of going out alone," I confided to him. But, in my mind, I was thinking about who I should recruit to form a team since the company was going under.

"I would be interested in joining you," Jim jumped in enthusiastically, interrupting my thoughts. "I was always interested in having my own business."

I was surprised to hear his response. Jim's background was in political science and government, including being a town manager in Boxford, a small town north of Boston, and he had worked at the State House in Boston too. He had left the government and joined the company in its real estate division, but he didn't have any technical background, and that concerned me. However, he was so eager. I suggested a few other potential people for our team, but Jim didn't think we needed additional partners. After all, I needed a partner, and he had a good character. So, after some consideration, I finally agreed.

By then, ADMN had bought a building and moved from Copley Square in Boston to an old, dilapidated building, previously a printing company, across from the Cambridge City Hall in Central Square. Central Square was rundown, vastly different from the grand and fashionable Copley Square. In the Central Square office, the team was separated into management on the third floor and the rest of the group in a dingy basement, which was incredibly demoralizing. The rest of the building was rented out. The downfall of ADMN was apparent.

Jim and I started formulating a business plan over long walks and lunches at a cafe near the Charles Hotel in Harvard Square. I would be CEO/president, and Jim would be executive vice president—just the two of us.

Over our lunches and working on our business plan together, I realized that Jim was very organized and could bring unique skills in marketing and communications. For example, he came up with how to create sleek marketing brochures. We complemented each other well.

I also thought he was probably the nicest person I'd ever met and a gentleman. I didn't know how old he was, but I knew he was much younger than me.

~~

In June 1988, we left ADMN and started our own company: Harvard Design and Mapping Co., Inc. (HDM) in Cambridge, Massachusetts—the heart of technology innovation.

It was a humble beginning with just Jim and me, without a contract or financial resources—only determination to make it on our own and a strong will to survive. For six months we lived on unemployment checks from the previous company since they had laid off most of the staff by then.

A bank refused a loan, asking for collateral. I was in the middle of a divorce and had no assets. After some brainstorming, Jim borrowed $50,000 from his aunt and I borrowed $50,000 from my sister with the condition that we would pay back with interest. We opened a certificate of deposit (CD) with that money, which became our collateral.

It took us over two years to repay the loan in installments whenever we could afford it. They were the company's first investors, and we felt good that we kept our promises.

I am an immigrant Asian woman. I had many disadvantages to overcome. However, we had pioneering, cutting-edge technology in geographic information systems.

The first job was from the Town of Kingston, Massachusetts, digitizing their assessors' maps and renumbering the archaic old parcels into computers. It was the early days of digitization, and they were one of the first towns to computerize maps and databases. With Jim's background in government and mine in technology, it was a successful project, and the customer was happy.

The second job was from the U.S. Coast Guard, computerizing their geographic assets, such as the location of lighthouses and even buoys, and computerizing its database around the country, automating their asset management system. It was a competitive bid, and we learned later that we beat many big companies because our proposal was concise and right to the point.

Once we signed the contract, I went to see the contracting officer on Governor's Island in New York. He asked, "Your company name, Harvard Design and Mapping, is familiar. How long have you been in business?"

"We are a relatively new company." But I didn't say we were a brand-new company. When naming the company, I read in a book to use the familiar sounding New England town names. It was perfect since I lived in the town of Harvard, and I thought "Harvard" was such a familiar name with connotations of quality and excellence due to the reputation of Harvard University—it seemed like my thinking had paid off!

Because of our trailblazing technology, we had no competition in the early days and were growing rapidly. However, we were still bootstrapping.

Those early days of HDM were particularly busy. One night I stayed late, almost until midnight, to finish work. I was exhausted. It was late fall, dark and drizzling. On the long drive home, over thirty miles, to Harvard, I missed a utility hole repair sign in the middle of the street on Concord Avenue, Cambridge. The blinking warning lights were broken, and I didn't see it with the glare until the last minute. Then, I swerved quickly to avoid it and hit a big oak tree at the corner of the intersection at full speed.

I temporarily lost consciousness, but somehow, an ambulance came and took me to the emergency room at nearby Mount Auburn Hospital in Cambridge. Unfortunately, my manual drive Saab was totaled. Thankfully, I was wearing a seatbelt and survived the crash. Around 2 a.m., after a thorough examination by a doctor, the nurse said, "You are being discharged. Who should I call to take you home?"

I lived too far away to call a taxi, and Katherine had just gone off to college. It came as a profound realization that I was all alone and had nobody to call. So, I asked the nurse to call Jim. The phone woke him up, and he came to the hospital and took me to his house in Melrose, where he lived with his parents. I spent a few days there recovering from the injury. I was in his younger sister's room, who had left for college. I remember thinking she had the same French-style white furniture as Katherine. Jim was attentive and incredibly caring, bringing me cups of tea and checking in on me constantly. The contrast between Jim and Kim was more than day and night.

~~~

I was in my mid-forties when we started the business together, and Jim was barely thirty. But he was mature for his age, and his mannerisms made him seem older. I liked him very much because he was caring and a true gentleman. Still, we had a significant age difference, and I pushed away any idea of a relationship other than a business partner. Besides, after lengthy, bitter divorce proceedings, I didn't want a relationship with anyone. I tried to introduce him to lovely young women from the previous company so I would forget any intimate feelings toward him.

However, we worked together for long hours, even on weekends. Jim was single, never married, and I was alone with my children away in college—Kevin at Carnegie Mellon in Pittsburgh and Katherine at Vassar College in Poughkeepsie. Sometimes, we took a break on weekends and went shopping at flea markets, which we both enjoyed—I still miss those New England antique markets!

Jim was born in Medford, outside of Boston, Massachusetts. He was the first to attend college in his family and the oldest son of six children to an Irish mother and English father. Jim was like his dad—kind and gentle, six foot tall with blue eyes and curly blond hair. While all the other siblings left the house, Jim stayed living with his parents to care for them.

A few years after we started the company, Jim moved out of his parent's home and rented an apartment in Belmont,

closer to work. Even though his parents were in their six-
ties and still functioning well, it created quite an anxiety
among his siblings, and eventually, his younger sister and
a brother, who lived locally, shared some responsibilities
with frequent visits to their parents.

Occasionally, when we worked late hours, he invited
me to stay at his apartment overnight instead of making
the long drive home.

After I asked for a divorce, it was a terrible time for
me. Kim was there waiting for me when I came home late
at night. He did many terrible things, like stalking. I was
often afraid for my life because he was mentally unstable.
At that stage, Jim would follow me in the car home—a
long drive—to ensure I got in safely. Jim and I grew much
closer over this time.

After the divorce in 1991, I sold the Harvard home
to buy a smaller place closer to work where my children
could come and stay. Jim and I discussed purchasing a
house together, which made sense economically. We started
looking for a place in Belmont, next to Cambridge.

We found an old single-family, two-story colonial home
with four symmetrical gable roofs, built in the late 1800s.
The price was right; it was the cheapest house in Belmont's
market. It needed tons of work—it had a leaking roof,
peeling paint, dingy old carpets, and century-old wallpaper—no doubt as to why it stayed on the market for so
long. However, the location was perfect on a nice-sized
corner lot, with four bedrooms where my children could
come and stay.

Jim and I had a long time getting to know each other—it
had been such a difficult time with my divorce, and I guess

we were both treading carefully. Plus, Jim was very protective of me. However, buying the Belmont house cemented our relationship and made it clear that Jim and I would be together. We took on the challenge of renovating the house. First, we redesigned and created the master bedroom with a bath, breaking down the wall of two adjoining bedrooms—the four bedrooms became three. Next, we lifted the wall-to-wall carpets, and to our surprise, we found lovely, rare, yellow pine floors underneath. I thought back, many years ago now, to discovering the exquisite oriental wallpaper underneath the ugly green one in the bedroom of the Harvard house. Sometimes, the most precious things are hidden below the surface, just waiting to be discovered.

We hired a French carpenter, a part-time blues musician at one of the clubs in Cambridge, whom we met while he was doing the carpentry work at our office building.

After six months of hard work, Jim and I transformed the house. We created a beautiful home for ourselves—a new brown architectural asphalt shingle roof, eggshell yellow exterior paint, landscaping with several Rose of Sharon bushes to screen the front porch from the street, a master bedroom with a modern ensuite bathroom, gleaming yellow pine floors, the old wallpaper replaced with dove white paint, and the other bathroom redone with new fixtures. We ran out of money and stopped there. We would do the kitchen later.

My children loved the house, the proximity to the city, and the public transit. Furthermore, they liked Jim. And our friends and families visited us more often, which is one thing that happens when you live near the city and with a nice man, it seems!

However, the business grew, and we wanted a bigger place to entertain guests and friends. So, a year later, we sold the house on our own—we both were excellent at this since Jim, too, had a real estate broker's license.

We made a sizable profit and searched for a new house on weekends. We soon realized Belmont was too expensive, so we went out further and eventually found a big, relatively new two-story colonial home in the historic town of Concord. It was in a desirable neighborhood of twenty-four homes in a gated community called Wright Farm, with a community swimming pool and tennis court. It was once a horse farm. Somehow, we were soon known in the neighborhood as "the *people who were never home*" because we worked long hours and traveled a lot for our growing business.

~~

On Columbus Day in 1994, we were married at the historic Lyman Estate in Waltham, witnessed by over eighty friends and family members. However, many of our business clients didn't know we were married until a *Boston Globe* article came out on our company. At the end of the interview, the Globe reporter asked me, "What does your husband do?"

I answered, anticipating the surprise, "We work together. My partner, Jim, is my husband."

She was so surprised and didn't know how to respond. Of course, she put that in the article, which became a public announcement of our marriage, surprising many clients who had no idea. After the article's publication, I received many phone calls. Another part of the article that caught the readers' attention was the reference to the ping pong games we played early in the morning before work, with a dollar bet for each contest, a source of my competitive spirit.

I often think I would never be where I am today if I hadn't divorced Kim. And I also believe I couldn't have gone through the divorce and built the business without Jim's support.

For a long time, I had the habit of looking for Jim at night, trying to touch him like a blind person looking for someone. I wanted to ensure he was still there.

I thought about how it all started. I think I know. Early in our marriage, I had nightmares of being chased violently, waking up screaming and in a sweat. Jim comforted me, saying *everything is alright*. He is always there for me for security and comfort.

CLOSURE

"Dad died." A 3 a.m. call from my daughter, Katherine, woke me up. It was on Sunday, August 11, 2019. She was calm. I let her talk for over an hour.

"I took a pill to control my nerves." She usually takes a pill for her flight anxiety.

She said, "I was about to take off at LAX for Portland, for a couple of days of R & R and to bring Eitan back home." (My grandson had been visiting family friends.)

"The plane was supposed to take off around 9 p.m. but was delayed to 9:30 p.m., then to 10:40 p.m., and so on," Katherine continued. "While waiting for the plane, I called Dad, but there was no answer, so I kept calling. Then I got a call from his caretaker who lives down the street from Dad."

The caretaker had told Katherine that her father's car windows had been left open for three days and asked if she'd like her to check on him. The caretaker had found him face-down on the bedroom floor with an empty liquor bottle strewn nearby. She got scared, ran out, and called Katherine back.

"Something was very wrong. I called Ben at the airport to go over and see what happened. Ben found him dead. He told me not to go there, as it would be too traumatic for me to see him like that, and he would call the funeral home," Katherine said.

How sad of an ending of one's life! In the end, he drank himself to death.

I called my brother, Kiseo, who also lives in L.A., in the morning, and he said he would contact Katherine in the afternoon after church. He knows the Korean funeral customs. I also called my sister, Kisoo, in Long Island, informed her of his death, and asked her to pray for his soul. The day was Sunday, and everyone in her family goes to church.

My ex-husband had moved closer to Katherine and his grandchildren in Los Angeles about three years earlier. He'd spent almost thirty years before that—since our divorce—living a somewhat reclusive life in Western Massachusetts. Katherine got closer to him when he moved to the L.A. area, and he was nice to his grandchildren, especially the younger ones, Dahlia and Eitan, who also got to know him better.

When Katherine told me he was moving to L.A., I was afraid of the encounters I had avoided for all these years, and I didn't want to bring back any old memories. The wound still felt raw sometimes. My siblings and I also worried about the disruptions he would cause to her marriage. Kim was never easy to deal with—there was always a destructive element to him, and people were never comfortable in his presence. We didn't want this to affect Katherine's relationship with her husband, Ben. Nevertheless, she welcomed him.

Having Kim move to Los Angeles impacted the relationship between me and Katherine. Even though she handled it very well, there was a bit of a strain at the same time, and my visits to her became more cautious and infrequent. However, a part of me was glad he could spend his last years near his daughter and grandchildren and wasn't alone.

Katherine mentioned her father had been in and out of the hospital lately, but I wasn't sure if his problem was mental or physical. Nonetheless, the news was still shocking to me. He was almost docile sometimes but violent and crazy at other times.

Even before Kim died, Katherine would call crying that he refused to take the doctor's medication for his mental condition and checked himself out of the hospital. She eventually thought he had bipolar disorder. I often thought he might have had schizophrenia. Throughout my marriage, I tried to analyze what was wrong with him but ultimately gave up.

I didn't know what to say, but I knew she needed me to listen to her.

"Did you call your brother Kevin?" I finally asked.

"Yes, I did. But I don't think he is coming." My heart sank.

Katherine broke down when I called her the following day to see how she was doing and if Kevin was with her. She was all alone grieving. She hesitated to ask for my help because she knew I had many painful memories of him. However, I told her that I would come out to help her.

She called about an hour later, having calmed down, and said, "You caught me in a terrible moment. I am better now. You don't have to come. It will stir up all your unpleasant memories."

I told her that Jim and I would help even if we could just be there.

A few days later, Jim and I hastily arranged the trip to L.A. and bought a one-way ticket from Nantucket to Los Angeles without knowing how long we needed to stay. We didn't even know when and where the funeral would be.

When we arrived at Katherine's house, she wore a long black dress. She had lost weight since we saw her a few months ago. The house was quiet. Only Eitan (eleven) was home with her. He had severed a tendon in his foot a week before and was still recovering. Dahlia had recently returned from a cooking camp in Connecticut but had already left again to work as a junior counselor at another summer camp. A few days earlier, Miles had gone to Berkeley to start his summer job, and Ben was working.

We were glad that we came. Katherine needed us. I asked how we could help, and she asked if we could shuttle Dahlia back and forth to camp and be with Eitan during the day so that she could take care of the funeral arrangements, which we did. We also took the kids out for back-to-school shopping, clothes for Dahlia, school supplies, and a new backpack for Eitan. They were delighted. They were afraid to ask their grieving mom.

Katherine was so bereft that there was almost no opportunity to share my feelings about the situation. I didn't want to interfere with her suffering, but I also didn't want her to be overwhelmed by emotion. Most of all, I worried about her and tried to listen carefully to her unresolved feelings.

Partly, I was very sorry for Kim's life, but simultaneously, I felt numb. I didn't know what I was feeling. It was a complex emotion and felt like a delicate balance. I told her that I was very sorry she had to go through the grieving alone without anyone to share, and genuinely, I wanted Kim to be sent off in a dignified way—that was important to me.

Katherine was a good daughter, dealing with her dad with patience and love, and she will have no regrets because she did her best. I am glad he spent time with her and his grandchildren nearby and didn't die alone.

Katherine told me he had set up a trust and will, and took her to meet his bankers and lawyer before he died. He must have known the end was near. He left all his inheritance to Kevin and Katherine equally. Even though his life was difficult, he planned things very carefully.

One evening, after dinner at a Korean restaurant in Koreatown, Jim took the kids home early in his rental car, and Katherine and I came home later and talked while sitting in her car. She was somewhat uncomfortable with Jim's presence in this situation and asked why he came and why I always said "we" rather than "I."

"We trust each other and do things together," I said.

She later told me what I said profoundly impacted her marriage and her own thoughts.

Jim and I came back to Nantucket after five days in L.A. I told Katherine that I would attend the funeral and burial.

The funeral was set at 11 a.m., Saturday, August 31st, in White House Junction, New Jersey. It was a clear, sunny day with the perfect temperature of low 70s—a blessing for the departed. I took an early morning flight from Nantucket to JFK. My nephew Joe and my sister Kisoo, who lived in Long Island, were waiting to pick me up upon arrival. The plane was on time, and we arrived at the funeral relatively early because the traffic was light.

Joe repeatedly mentioned how much he appreciated what Kevin had done during *Imo*'s (aunt) illness. Several years ago, my sister Kisoo was very sick in New York University Hospital's Intensive Care Unit with septic shock. Kevin, living in Manhattan, kept vigil every day at the hospital. Good deeds come around when you need them most.

When we arrived, Kevin, his wife Annie, Katherine, her husband Ben, and all three grandchildren, Miles, Dahlia, and Eitan, were at the funeral home's door. When Eitan saw us at the funeral home's parking lot, he ran to us and hugged me tightly. No more braces. His severed tendon seemed all healed. He didn't recognize Joe or my sister Kisoo, but he was happy to see them and gave them big hugs, too. He looked handsome in a dark suit and tie.

Kevin and Katherine had arranged the funeral on their own, with no one from Kim's side of the family around except his oldest nephew, Geunsoo, who had flown in from Korea to represent the families in Korea. I saw him last when he came to the U.S. to Graduate School at Carnegie Mellon over thirty years ago, and now he was beyond middle age.

The funeral was a small gathering but well attended. Katherine's college friend, Alexa, accompanied by her children; Sarabinh, Ben's cousin and Katherine's classmate from Boston; and Kevin's good college friend Norm from DC, came. My old friend from Clinton, NJ, Helen Devaney—Father John Devaney's mother—and her two daughters, Eileen and Sheila, attended the funeral, burial, and dinner afterward. Sheila is Katherine's oldest friend. They were born two weeks apart. Her family lived across the street from us on Hillside Drive in Clinton. Of course, my sister Kisoo and nephew Joe were also there with me. Father John Devaney, my godson, a Dominican priest, officiated the funeral. Father John said he could not do the church funeral because Kim was not baptized. Nevertheless, it was a beautiful funeral and burial service.

Of course, Ben and Annie stood by and worked hard—it was tough for them, too. The casket was closed under the unusual circumstances of the funeral occurring over twenty days after his death. Korean customs also don't have open caskets.

I met Kim's old friend and colleague from RCA and his wife, the only friend who attended the funeral. I didn't remember his name, but I remembered Kim used to go to his house to play poker every Saturday night. So, I asked him about others at his work whom I used to know, and he said he could not remember them, but some had died, some were not in good health, and some even had Alzheimer's.

It was the 1970s when we lived in New Jersey. We were young then. Time went by.

One conversation I had with him struck me. He said his children fondly remembered Kim bringing candies whenever he came to his house. It hit me with sadness because he never showed that kind of tenderness to his own children. Why?

Kevin gave the eulogy; his father asked him to come before he died, but he didn't. He reflected on his decision, and he didn't seem to regret not being able to see him before he died. It was a heart-aching eulogy about their troubled relationship, a father-and-son relationship he never had.

He also reflected on funny moments of what his father was like—buying ten bunches of scallions simply because they were on sale, even though he couldn't use them all. And when Kevin introduced Annie to his dad, he first said, "Let's buy the lottery tickets together." Forever a gambler. However, he worked hard for his family in his capacity, and despite his drinking problem, he never missed work.

He wished to be buried at the Fairmont Cemetery in New Jersey. He'd told Katherine that living in New Jersey was his best and happiest time. Was I happy, too, then? Life with him somehow always felt in turmoil.

At the burial, his nephew, Geunsoo, from Korea, bowed to the coffin, kneeling on the ground as is the Korean custom: two with his head to the ground and a third, with a half bow. Kevin, Katherine, and Ben followed him kneeling in the same way.

I shoveled dirt on the coffin, finally let go of all my hard feelings, and said a final goodbye. In the end, I did forgive him. He can no longer harm anybody. I wished him Godspeed on his way and the peace that comes from good closure. I tried to imagine his final days and felt sad.

I didn't cry but finally broke down at my babies' tombs. After all those years, Kim had brought Kenneth's remains from Indiana and reburied him beside Karen. Kenneth must have been in his mind all along, just like Kenneth was in mine all these times. Kim was buried several yards down the slope near the cemetery's eastern edge.

It had been a brilliantly sunny day, yet suddenly, the weather turned quite windy despite it being August, like his turbulent life.

His obituary read, "Mr. Simyung Kim, age 83, passed away on August 7, 2019, in his favorite armchair at home in Tujunga, California. Funeral services will be held at 11:00 a.m. on Saturday, August 31, 2019, at the Kearns Funeral Home in Whitehouse, New Jersey. He will rest in a private burial at the Fairmont Cemetery, 256 Old Turnpike Road, Califon, New Jersey, alongside his two beloved babies, Kenneth and Karen. May he rest in peace."

MOTHER'S DAY

May 2018

I panicked that I'd forgotten to send flowers to my mom on Mother's Day. But then, I realized that she had passed away a year earlier.

Her birthday was on April 14th on the moon calendar, which usually comes a month later on the Gregorian calendar and is often close to Mother's Day. So, my youngest brother Kiseo, who lived in L.A. and was my mother's favorite son, and I shared responsibilities, sending flowers on her birthday and Mother's Day. We rotated so that it wouldn't overlap. She loved the flowers and always had some on her windowsill.

She had been in a nursing home in Flushing, New York, for many years. Her room had a window overlooking Manhattan's skyline, and I would lie down on her bed with her and share stories and laughter.

I remembered her table at the dining hall, even though her tablemates had changed many times over the years.

Sometimes, coming off the elevator, I found her sitting by the nurse's station among other women residents. She despised them at the beginning of her time there, saying they all had Alzheimer's. When she saw me, her eyes opened wide, she pointed at me, and exclaimed, "She is my daughter, my younger daughter!" Even though almost everyone there knew me already, she still wanted to introduce me proudly.

If I told Mom I was coming, she would count the days and hours until my arrival. And, if anything happened where I had to cancel my visit, I could feel her disappointment. Afterward, I decided to call her while driving down from Boston. When we were about an hour from her place, I surprised her so she didn't have to wait too long to see me.

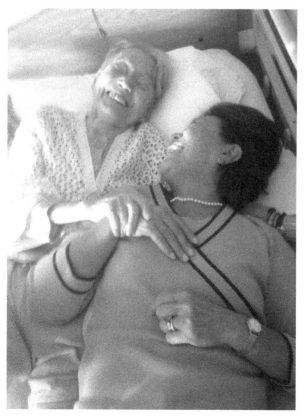

Figure 9. My Mom and I share a laugh

On one of my visits, I left Jim and Mom alone in the room while I went to the nurse's station to get an update about her condition. When I returned, she declared happily, "Jim and I had a good conversation!" I looked at Jim and interpreted what she had just said. And Jim said smiling, "Oh, yes. We did." Mom didn't speak English, and Jim didn't speak Korean. But I often found that mom talked to Jim at length in Korean, thinking he would understand every word she said.

On this Mother's Day, I celebrated with my daughter, Katherine, and granddaughter, Dahlia, in L.A., three generations of women, and I was thinking about my mother on this Mother's Day.

I missed her and missed sending her flowers because of her smile and the joy of her receiving them.

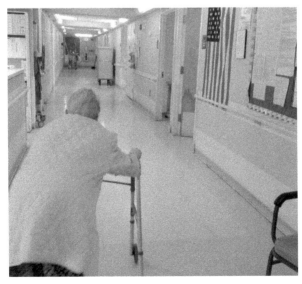

Figure 10. My Mother at the nursing home in New York

LIFE LESSONS
FROM MY PARENTS

I sang my mother's favorite hymns at her bedside, repeating like a replay of CDs. She was dying, having not recovered from a broken hip from a fall a few months earlier. Mom closed her eyes and listened. Perhaps she was thinking of the good old days when we children were little, singing hymns at home. That was my father's favorite thing. "Let's sing together." He often encouraged his children to join him in singing hymns.

My mother's specialty was prayer. She prayed for everyone and believed her prayers were always answered. We thought so, too. When someone was sick, grandkids needed to get into good schools, or an important exam was coming, we asked Mother to pray for us.

Several years after my father's death, my mother decided to join her children and came to America in the late 1970s, and we were reunited. She recollected how heartbroken she was when I left and said, "When you left for America, I thought of you every day, day after day, and month after month. I was sad and held my tears every mealtime, looking at an empty seat at the table. What a great country America is! I never thought I was going to see you again. Yet, here we are, reunited, thousands of miles away across the Pacific."

My mother had experienced separation before. She always longed for her sister, who was a mere few hundred miles away in North Korea, but was never able to see her again since Korea was divided into North and South after World War II.

Growing up in Korea, especially after the Korean War, money was tight. However, my parents always made their regular donations to the church. I complained when I needed a new uniform, "Mom, why don't you buy me a uniform instead of giving money to the church?" And she replied, "If you buy everything you want first, there won't be any money left to give to the church." Then, I no longer complained.

Years later, during my business trips, I often visited my mom in Los Angeles, where she first lived when she moved to America. I lamented once, "I am too busy running the business, being involved in nonprofit boards, and doing charity work. I should reduce the extra activities and focus on my business."

She sighed and advised, "You are lucky that people ask you to help them. They won't ask you anymore if you wait until you are not busy. They are asking you because they know busy people get things done. So, do it while you can." My mother wasn't college-educated, but she was well-read and wise.

My father loved and was proud of his children and his family. His steady encouragement and praise gave us children self-confidence. I have learned many lifelong lessons from my father. In particular, the importance of an authentic and loving family. As devout Christians, my parents also taught us the faith.

As an adult and a businesswoman, I often thought about the lessons I learned from my parents. As a result, I have done much charity work and learned more through those works than through my business alone.

In the early 1990s, I started the Silk Road Gala for the Asian Task Force Against Domestic Violence (ATASK) in Boston, raised significant funds for ATASK over the following decades, and served as the Board's chairperson for several years. I also served on the Board of Trustees of Clark University—I was the first foreign graduate school alum to serve on the board. Under my company's name, Harvard Design and Mapping Company (HDM), I established a fellowship for international doctoral students in geography. I was one of them a long time ago.

Those experiences enriched my life and helped build the solid professional network I lacked at the start of my business. Even years after my retirement, strangers approached me and remembered me from my charity work, especially for ATASK and the Silk Road Gala.

⌒⌒

My mother died peacefully in February 2017 in a nursing home in New York, surrounded by her children, their spouses, and grandchildren. She was just a couple of months shy of her 103rd birthday.

During my mother's last days, my brothers and sisters—five in all (we lost our youngest sister, Kimyung, in the early 1980s)—discussed what to do with our father's grave in Korea. Only one sibling, my sister Kiok, was still in Korea. The others were all in America. After Kiok was gone, no one would care for his grave. So, we decided to bring his remains to America and bury him with our mother. He never set foot in this country or saw his children's successes in America; however, he would now be coming here in ashes. He would have loved America!

In short order, Kiok worked hard in Korea for the disinterment of his grave, cremating his remains, getting a death record, and certifying all of it in English in the U.S. Embassy. Then, finally, she came to New York with his ashes on June 2, 2017, with her husband Sooil carrying the special urn in his backpack. Their son Janghan and her oldest grandson accompanied them for the reinterment.

Finally, forty-six years after his death, my father joined and was buried with my mother on Saturday, June 3rd, at 10:30 a.m., at the All Saints Church Cemetery in Great Neck, New York. It was a little over three months after my mother's death. His children and several grandchildren attended the ceremony, which my mother's favorite minister officiated. As life turned out, I hadn't returned to Korea. Instead, I brought my father to America.

The tombstone was engraved with my mother's and father's names in Korean and the same verses of the Psalms from his old tombstone in Korea: *Lord Almighty! How lovely is your dwelling place! I long to dwell in your house forever and take refuge in the shelter of your wings.*

TWO SUMMERS

June 2019 on Nantucket

A small upside-down saltbox house sits off the sandy road in the westernmost part of Nantucket Island. It is called "Harborside" and has been our summer home for twenty-six years. The shingles are all worn and gray, beaten by the harsh weather over the years. It is probably the smallest house on the block, yet it has the most beautiful garden, my pride and joy.

In the raised bed in the front, a variety of flowers are rotating in bloom: daffodils, irises, peonies, spireas, hydrangeas, Hawaiian hibiscus, and butterfly plants, among others. New Dawn pink roses climb to the roof. In August, our Rose of Sharon blooms with hundreds of deep pink flowers without fail, providing a stunning hedge on the western side of the yard. They are windswept sideways at almost a forty-five-degree angle.

The Rose of Sharon is the national flower of Korea, symbolizing its hardiness and endurance with its continuing bloom. No wonder they survive Madaket's harsh environment even though they are bent like an old man. A little bit of the old country in a summer home in my adopted country.

Standing amid this flower garden, I feel at peace. I feel at peace with my life. In the early years of my first marriage, I had a lot of regrets. *Why did I come here? Why didn't I stay in Korea?* Sometimes, I doubted God—*why did I have to go through all that I went through. What did I do to deserve this?* But now, I don't. How many women out there have success in both business and life itself?

However, it still bothers me that my children never knew a happy family growing up. I can't change the past, but I can control the future. I look forward.

I had such a caring family when I was growing up. Even though there was the war, and our family didn't have much money, we had loving parents. I wanted the same thing for

Figure 11. Flower garden at Harborside on Nantucket

my children. On some level, I think this is why I used to drag the kids to open houses every weekend—I was trying to find that perfect home where I could find happiness and stability for them—a daily life without turmoil.

Over the years, I have become a different person in certain ways. I think that "who I am" has evolved. However, in some ways, I've simply returned to my authentic self, the happy person I was, who had been lost—I had to find her again.

I'm more tolerant and more grateful for my life now than I ever could have been because of what I've been through. The hardships I experienced gave me a stronger foundation. And ultimately, life led me in a different

Figure 12. Rose of Sharon in the garden

direction, and I became a pioneering businesswoman in digital mapping technology.

I could never have imagined I would be a businessperson, but underlying ambition and fire were always there and have never been extinguished. Even during twenty years of a difficult first marriage, I never gave up wanting to be "somebody." If I met my younger self from where I am today, I'd say to her:

Don't give up, be confident, and always stay positive.

I had to chart my new life once it took a different road by simply taking one step at a time. I credit the supportive relationship with my husband Jim, for helping me on this journey.

Even though I don't go to church often, I still believe in my prayers being answered. When I encounter difficult things, I do pray. It's faith. My belief in God is there.

The viburnum, wild rose, and honeysuckle perfume the air in the back of the open field toward the harbor. I see a beautiful pair of cardinals and yellow finches on a cherry tree. It is truly a small piece of paradise.

We love Madaket for its unspoiled natural beauty, the island's remote, quiet, and unassuming nature, and beautiful beaches where we walk for miles and miles. The upstairs deck off the living room looks over Madaket Harbor and beyond to magnificent sunsets over Tuckernuck Island. The best part of the evening! Jim used to call it *our mental health clinic.* The beauty and solitude kept us sane and healthy during those hectic days of running our business.

On September 9, 2023, I read an accolade in a magazine about Castronovo Chocolate Factory in Jupiter, Florida, founded by a young woman who used to work for me. I sent her a congratulatory note.

She immediately responded, "Thank you, Kija! It is so nice to hear from you! You were such an inspiration for my entrepreneurship!"

I hope I can inspire many more women through my memoir.

When running the company, I often spoke to working women audiences to inspire them in their careers. It was these women who encouraged me to write my stories. What I have learned about writing is that I need to be brutally honest, no matter how painful it is. Writing this memoir became a healing process for me.

~~

One of my fondest memories as a little child was at my father's farm in Yeoncheon, about thirty miles north of Seoul. Before the Korean War, we spent summers there every year. There was a river where children played and swam, and women washed their clothes. The farm and the rice fields stretched from the river to the mountains on the other side. My favorite part was the peach orchard next to our farmhouse, where my boy cousin and I spent many hours roaming and discovering.

I longed for a place where my children and grandchildren would have lasting memories like my father's farm, and here on Nantucket, our children and grandchildren can't wait to come in the summertime. They will fondly remember crabbing, clamming, catching minnows, riding the surf, and biking. And, of course, the midnight walks for stargazing, too.

Figure 13. Dahlia flying a kite at Madaket Beach

For so many years, I thought the peach orchard and my childhood summers were just a memory. And yet, here I am again, in another summer, another garden, maybe more beautiful than the first.

Figure 14. Catching minnows; from left to right: Jim, Dahlia, and Eitan

AFTERWORD:
My Letter to Readers

Initially, I thought I would write a book about my business. When running my software company in Cambridge, Massachusetts, I used to do a fair amount of public speaking, especially to working women audiences. Many of them encouraged me to write my stories, which had inspired them in their own lives and careers. So, after my retirement, I spent many years toying with the idea of writing a memoir. I thought the business would be the most significant part of my story. But really, it's only been a dent.

Finally, in 2014, I met with a writing coach, Clare McFadden, introduced by a neighbor and a friend, Nancy Sommers. Nancy is an English professor at Harvard University, and Clare was her former student. Clare and I met at a cafe in Harvard Square to discuss the structure my story might take. Clare asked me to write a five-hundred-word essay to begin. I wrote one page of bullet points covering my life. When she asked me for more details, saying she had many questions, I said I couldn't remember much, especially about my childhood. However, she did not accept this as an answer.

Over the coming weeks and years, it turned out that there were many stories I wanted to tell. It was surprising to me how much I could remember. For instance, I didn't think I could remember much about the Korean War at all—I was only a child!—however, when I sat down to write, the memories came flooding back. So, for anyone reading this who has thought about writing a memoir but just can't start, I encourage you to sit down and write—the stories will come.

The success story is straightforward, and it's the end game. But bringing the sad stories of my life to the surface was very difficult. However, I discovered it was almost like redemption. I couldn't write many of my sad stories at the start of this work. They were buried deep down, and I didn't want to disturb them. But once they started coming to the surface, it was very healing for me.

In the early stories, I was crying as I wrote. Now, I don't cry anymore. Before, I never wanted to share these stories. I was very timid about writing that part of my story. I was not ashamed, but it was too painful to share. However, I've shared some stories with my writers groups. They encouraged me to keep writing more about survival during a terrible war in Korea, the personal perseverance, the thoughts, feelings, and the drive it took to become a successful businesswoman, an immigrant in a place that did not share my customs, language, or history. And now, I want to share it! It's such a healing process.

Thank you for reading my story,
Kija

ACKNOWLEDGMENTS

I must first thank Clare McFadden, my writing coach, formerly from Harvard University. She is the most patient person dealing with the most impatient person, me. Without her, this memoir wouldn't exist.

Thanks to my three writers groups: Nantucket Writers Group, Women's Cultural Alliances (WCA) of Naples Memoir Writing Group, and Naples Writers Forum of Florida. They offered me countless hours of constructive criticism and suggestions and encouraged me to keep writing.

Thanks to Judy Isserlis from the WCA Memoir Writing group. Judy read my story on "Summer of 1966" and found, through her genealogy research tool, my first American friend, Kevin Geuther, living in Delray Beach, Florida, with whom I had lost touch for over fifty-five years. What a miracle! Kevin kept her name, Geuther, which made the search possible, and she was healthy at ninety! When I saw her again, she said, "Stars must have been realigned for our reunion!"

My husband, Jim Aylward, read many of my stories and helped me with research materials and photos.

I also owe my gratitude to my brother, Kigap Sohn, and sister, Kisoo Shim, who answered numerous phone calls to refresh my memories and helped me recollect many childhood events.

Thanks to my niece, Dr. Holly Kim, who read my stories early on and encouraged me despite her hectic schedule.

I thank my two children, Kevin and Katherine, who believed in me and gave me strength when I needed it most.

ABOUT THE AUTHOR

 KIJA KIM is an award-winning entrepreneur and businesswoman.

Born in Seoul, Korea, she came to America in 1966 to attend the Graduate School of Geography at Clark University in Worcester, Massachusetts, and has lived in the U.S. ever since.

Kija founded the Harvard Design and Mapping Company (HDM) in Cambridge in 1988, when women ran only 1 percent of software firms in Massachusetts. She has been active in business and Asian communities and served in the Massachusetts Asian American Commission, the nation's first such commission, for twenty years. She was also the founder of the Silk Road Gala, an annual fundraising event for the Asian Task Force Against Domestic Violence and served as its board chair for many years. Kija was a member of the Republic of Korea Taskforce for the Three-Year Plan for Economic Innovation, appointed in 2014 by South Korea's President, Park Geun-Hye.

Kija resides in Naples, Florida, with her husband and has two grown children and three grandchildren.

Meridian is her first book.